THE WAY
OF JESUS

The Way of Jesus

To Repair and Renew the World

Bruce Chilton

Abingdon Press
Nashville

THE WAY OF JESUS
TO REPAIR AND RENEW THE WORLD

Library of Congress Cataloging-in-Publication Data

Chilton, Bruce.
    The way of Jesus : to repair and renew the world / Bruce Chilton.
        p.   cm.
    ISBN 978-1-4267-0006-4 (pbk. : alk. paper)
    1. Jesus Christ—Person and offices. 2. Healing—Religious aspects—Christianity. 3. Soul—Christianity. I. Title.
    BT205.C49 2010
    232—dc22

                                                                        2009022181

Translations of the Holy Bible and the Qur'an are the author's originals.

10 11 12 13 14 15 16 17 18 19—10 9 8 7 6 5 4 3 2 1

MANUFACTURED IN THE UNITED STATES OF AMERICA

Contents

To Begin

Jesus has influenced human societies on every continent in profound ways. His influence continues to move the hearts of billions of people around the world. Generations of thinkers—theologians, of course, but also philosophers and historians, social activists and artists of every faith (including atheism)—have thought hard about who Jesus truly was.

I have been involved in discussing Jesus and his impact for most of my life; the entire range of issues still fascinates me.[1] Scholars assess the available evidence, reflect on how they can come to conclusions, debate how to weigh one claim over another, and sometimes disagree with the cut and thrust of words honed to sharp edges. Amidst all that exciting intellectual activity, I have grown increasingly aware of what the study of Jesus too often misses.

Captivating though Jesus remains as a person, his basic message was not about himself. One reason there continues to be debate about Jesus' identity is that for the most part he didn't insist on a single definition of who he was; he did not teach a creed or spell out doctrines. Other things concerned him more.

Those of us who are interested in Jesus have perhaps become too involved in our arguments and investigations. We might give more attention to a fundamental issue: what did Jesus want to accomplish during his life? Understanding Jesus' goal and purpose will naturally shed light on how he thought of himself, but his aims are crucial in their own terms. Jesus' aims put into place the actions, the attitudes, and the sources of energy and inspiration that have motivated generations of men, women, and children to change the world around them for the better part of two millennia. Whatever their particular beliefs, people moved by Jesus' example have been moving forces of transformation.

This book is about the forces Jesus wanted to unleash in people in order to make change happen. He took on that task because he stood in the lineage of prophets who came before him, just as he inspired many prophetic figures who came after him. Whoever else Jesus was, he was—as he said and many people in his time recognized—a prophet. Attention to his prophetic purpose, which for reasons I'll explain I have called *to repair and renew the world*, will bring home to us truths about Jesus that are deeper than our disagreements over how to identify him.

The prophetic impulse itself, of course, predates Jesus by millennia. The desire to learn divine wisdom, and to translate its beauty and order and power into the affairs of human beings features as a primordial ambition in many ancient cultures. Moses, who lived over a thousand years before Jesus, was nonetheless the premier prophet of Jesus' culture. One dimension of Moses' teaching is essential to appreciate in order to grasp Jesus' intention. For Jesus, as for Moses, prophecy should not be thought of as an attainment for only a select few; God intends to broaden the horizon of prophecy far beyond the limitations people commonly place on which individuals should be addressed as "prophet."

Within a vivid scene in the book of Numbers, Moses says to his followers (Numbers 11:29), "Who will grant that all the LORD's people are prophets, that he will put his Spirit upon them?" His words speak on two levels.

At one level, this exasperated question is driven by circumstance. In Numbers 11, Israel in the wilderness is recalcitrant, complaining to Moses that they preferred the foods of Egypt to the miraculous bread they eat on the way to the land of promise. Sustained by the miracle of the *manna* that is available to them every day, all they can do is discourage one another with the recollection of the rich fare they used to enjoy. They compound their collective, morale-sapping nostalgia with their recollection that the food was free. No doubt it was—for the very good reason that the Hebrews were *slaves* in Egypt. Their masters had no choice but to feed them. Moses sees the Israelites' nostalgia for slavery, and realizes they are too refractory for him to lead into the land promised them.

Dispirited and feeling beyond the limit of his strength, Moses complains to his LORD that he cannot bear the weight of guiding people who have become too heavy for him. But the LORD finds a way to help. He promises to put his Spirit upon seventy elders, to augment prophetic leadership, easing Moses' burden. When God gave his Spirit, an additional two elders, who were not with the group immediately gathered around Moses, also began prophesying. Joshua, Moses' assistant, complained about that—concerned that Moses' role as leader would be eclipsed. But as far as Moses was concerned, more prophets were necessary as well as permissible; only their addition could permit him and the Israelites to continue.

Moses literally replies to Joshua in Hebrew, as in the rendering given here, "Who will grant that all the LORD's people are prophets?" In other words, Moses tells Joshua not to stand in God's way with a limited and limiting understanding of prophecy. English translations typically read here, "I wish that all the LORD's people were prophets," or "Would that all the LORD's people were prophets." Those renderings miss the point by making the statement too wishful. Moses is stating that he *knows* the LORD will provide all the prophets needed to guide his people, and that what stands between more prophecy and Israel is not God's will but human resistance.

At a second level, deeper than the particular circumstances involved, Moses articulated a fundamental truth about the entire biblical tradition, and about many cultures influenced by the Bible. Although there are indeed great prophets whose attainments make them authoritative teachers and guides of the community, in principle God is generous with his Spirit and wants to spread it among all his people.

Belief in the grounding generosity that makes God spread his Spirit unites the Abrahamic traditions. In Christianity, the Spirit of God enters every single believer at the moment of baptism, just as that Spirit entered Jesus, offering guidance and strength for the rest of one's life. A teaching of Islam (in a hadith related by Muhammad's wife Aisha, and recorded by Al-Bukhari) holds that when a Muslim recites the Qur'an precisely, the believer will, like Muhammad, be in the company of the noble and obedient angels. Moses' aspiration for all God's people to become prophets speaks for the Abrahamic religions as a whole, not only for Judaism.

Similarities in belief obviously do not mean that these religions have found enduring concord. The history of their conflicts is often violent and tragic. I have written elsewhere of how they share, not only profound truths of God, but also distorted justifications of violence that have proven incalculably destructive.[2] Ignoring those strategies of inflicting harm under the name of martyrdom is dangerous, because they are all the more influential the less they are openly acknowledged. But the Abrahamic inheritance also includes the most powerful, transformative, and healing strength that there has ever been: prophecy.

All three faiths, in their differing ways, intend that prophecy should be a universal, human inheritance, rather than the preserve of an elite—or even the prerogative of just one kind of faith. They see that prophetic engagement will change the world, and have developed visions of what that transformation will be like. For Islam, it is a matter of renewal (*tajdid*), a return to the pristine state of humanity, when people lived as intended by Allah. In Judaism, prophetic action brings about the *tiqqun 'olam*, the repair of the world's wounds. Christianity anticipates a final judgment (*parousia* in Greek) when Jesus himself will be the standard of a justice that vindicates human gentleness against all the violence of this world.

The differences among these visions of the goal and end of prophetic renewal are important and merit serious attention.[3] Just as ignoring the false justification of violence in the Abrahamic traditions serves to promote violence, so also the pretense that all religions are the same is fallacious. The simple fact is the final aim of the world—*tajdid, tiqqun,* or *parousia*—is described in profoundly different ways in Islam, Judaism, and Christianity. Attempts to overlook differences only produce deep disappointment, when believers of one tradition truly get to know believers of another tradition. The comparison of religions cannot be effective if it is based on the willing suspension of disbelief, which is a sound principle of the theater but a poor guide to understand the convictions that have guided human communities for millennia.

The differing ways in which the Abrahamic religions conceive of the aim and purpose of the world coincides with how they view the source of authority in the present. Islam looks to the Qur'an as the precise recitation of God's word, while Christians see Jesus as the embodiment of the divine word, God revealed in human flesh, and Rabbinic literature portrays the sages of Judaism as the teachers who continue the work of the elders with whom Moses shared the Spirit of God. Those great differences are only the beginning of the story of what separates the Abrahamic religions from one another, and multiple divisions *within* each tradition also need to be taken into account.

But alongside the recognition of deep differences, potential conflicts, and debates that are both bewildering and intriguing in their complexity, prophecy remains as a common, grounding force in the Abrahamic religions. Without ignoring what divides each tradition from the others, that commonality also demands our recognition. We should recognize the common recourse to prophecy out of simple honesty. Failing to acknowledge what unites as well as what divides religious traditions gets in the way of understanding.

In ethical terms, as well, the grounding importance of prophecy requires urgent attention. Judaism, Christianity, and Islam are in conflict today, or near to conflict, in many volatile settings throughout the world. The discovery of their common prophetic foundation can suggest ways in which they can *compete* and *coexist* with a sense of complementing one another, rather than attempting to exclude each other.

Yet the force of prophecy is by no means uniquely Abrahamic. For that reason, as this book proceeds and the prophetic inheritance is considered, I will draw on other religious traditions, as well. Often, another great tradition articulates best of all a feature of prophetic action that is present in the Abrahamic religion, without being fully explained. Buddhist, Hindu, and Taoist sources can teach everyone, including those of the Abrahamic faiths, about the nature of prophecy.

The breadth of prophecy in one form or another across religions is matched by its depth as a feature of human experience. There have been prophets ever since men and women believed that, while living in this world, they could see or hear or touch another reality, deeper and more substantial than what is experienced by sensory perceptions. Historians of religion have typically used the word "shaman" to describe this role in prehistoric and preliterate cultures.

The term "shaman" comes from Tungus, the language of Siberia and Manchuria, and refers to priests who function as mediums of the world of spirits by means of sacrifice, trance, music, storytelling, and healing. But "shaman" has then been applied to any such intermediary agent, in no matter what continent or period, between the natural and supernatural realms. From the leopard-skin priests of Southern Sudan to the Huichol peyote masters of Central Mexico, shamans past and present form a reminder that peoples in most places and most times have believed that the world we can see is not the whole of reality. Figures such as Deborah in the book of Judges (chapters 4 and 5) also fit the category: she sings, utters oracles, and lives in a cultic center where she also adjudicates disputes and guides the communities that consult her.

Belief in higher powers, beyond the constraints of the natural world, is basic to the development of religions as a whole, and the prophet—the human agent with shamanic powers—who is able to bridge the divide between the natural and supernatural is a characteristic figure of ancient art as well as ancient texts. That is the territory that prophecy negotiates, so that many religious traditions are in a position to shed light on what it means and feels like to be a prophet. To treat prophecy in one religion to the exclusion of others invites misunderstanding.

My starting point in this book is that Jesus' persona was that of a prophet, deeply rooted in the Judaism of his time. That historical finding leads on to another inquiry: how did Jesus see his prophetic powers mediated to other people so that they too became prophets? It would be possible to ask the same question of Moses and Muhammad, and other teachers of their stature.

The focus on Jesus does not suggest that only he achieved prophetic stature, or that only he intended to make his followers prophets. He is one way to see into the wisdom of how people become prophets. The way in which the Gospels, the principal sources about Jesus, present the prophetic vocation make them an especially rich source of wisdom, particularly when they are read comparatively, with other great religious literatures.

When we learn from Jesus as a source of prophetic wisdom, we need not take any prior position about him theologically or in terms of faith. Whether he is God's Son, how he is God's Son, and how any divine identity would comport with a truly human nature—these issues all figure as important questions within Christianity. But Jesus himself did not enter into discussion about any of these topics. Instead, he addressed his vigorous, prophetic message to the people of his generation and expected them to respond to God's call. At some point, that prophetic part of his message must be of interest to Christians of faith, and we are living at a time when the power of prophecy could prove a vital resource for human civilization as a whole, whatever one's starting point of belief.

The onset of the twenty-first century has been a great disappointment for many people around the world. Instead of prosperity and technological advance and relative calm after the end of the Cold

War, most every country in the world is gripped by unease as wealth appears insecure, the resources of well-being and civilization slip away from the grasp of many citizens, and wars between nations and within nations become daily reality. By comparison, it produces nostalgia, a rueful smile, or sorrow at the folly of human arrogance, to remember that at the end of the twentieth century, a book was written called *The End of History and the Last Man,* in which the author argued that his time marked "not just the end of the Cold War, or the passing of a particular period of postwar history, but the end of history as such: that is, the end point of mankind's ideological evolution and the universalization of Western liberal democracy as the final form of human government."[4] By a striking combination of his own resourcefulness and clever marketing, the same author continues to publish books as a "public intellectual."

History has neither ended nor reached a plateau. Profound uncertainty, punctuated by attempts to establish tyranny, by flights of excessive greed, but also by examples of generosity and courage, have become the order of our days. When human beings are uncertain, they rightly and naturally seek for enduring truths. That is part of what makes political tyrants appealing: the prospect of clear answers to all manner of complex social questions. In much the same way, uncertainty often breeds fixed ideologies, which promise solutions to life's problems on the basis of, say, Marxism, Fascism, Fundamentalism (of one sort or another), or nationalism. The beginning of the twenty-first century has been so disturbed, there is even an increase in the sort of racism in many parts of the world that would have seemed impossible in the years after the Second World War.

Although the result of embracing these false certainties is harmful and often tragic, that does not make the search for meaning or the human desire to overcome uncertainty illegitimate or unworthy. To the contrary: we need to identify and acknowledge the common impetus to discover meaning in the face of chaos so that it will become more difficult to exploit by the merchants of ideological quick fixes.

The Abrahamic faiths, considered in the light of global religious traditions, open the world of prophecy to us as the place where people confront what they are and can become, where meaning is realized, and where the strength to refashion the world may be found. Jesus will be our guide into this resource, which belongs as much to the constitution of humanity as to the foundation of faith.

Jesus introduced his prophetic principles by means of a coordinated set of themes. His coordination of primordial themes brought his vision as a prophet into a form that his disciples could readily understand. Jesus developed a precise model of prayer, today called the Lord's Prayer or the Paternoster, which speaks of how God relates to us. Taken down to its original Aramaic form, which the last section of this book ("Mindful Practice") will return to, Jesus wanted all his followers to pray:

'abba	(my) father/source
yitqadash shemakh	your name will be sanctified
tetey malkhutakh	your Kingdom will come
hav li yoma lakhma d'ateh	give me today the bread
ushebaq li yat chobati	that is coming
ve'al ta'eleyni lenisyona	and release me my debts
	not bring me to the test

The prayer of Jesus sets out ways of approaching God, calling upon him as father, looking for sanctification and the coming of his Kingdom, as well as asking for bread that is coming, debts to be forgiven, and the avoidance of any test that would show a believer to be disloyal.

Each of these addresses and petitions involves a way in which a human being responds to God, which we trace in the chapters that follow. God's power as father and creator brings the response of the Soul (chapter 1). The holiness of his name excites the answer of Spirit within human beings (chapter 2). The promise of his Kingdom pushes believers to realize divine justice in their lives (chapter 3). As people pray for bread each day, they also develop the insight to see that sustenance when it arrives (chapter 4). God's forgiveness is a force that develops new resources within each of us (chapter 5). And finally, coming to terms with how God judges us—releasing sin, and opening potentials for mercy (chapter 6) and glory (chapter 7)—provides strength for the continuing resilience of prophetic action.

The prophetic powers that Jesus intended to pass on to his followers are the inheritance, not merely of believers but of any person who wishes to understand him. They are pillars of humanity and the continuance of civilization that we can build upon, if we are patient enough to discern them. These are resources not only of belief but also of learning to become human with Jesus as a guide, and they identify powers within people—despite the variety and hardship of their conditions—that reside within them because they are God's children. They only await our recovering them so that we may repair and renew a broken world, starting with our broken selves.

1
Soul

Each and every one of us is earth.

Earth is not merely the planet we live on, or the environment we live in. Earth's seas flow in our veins, earth's soil nourishes us, and earth's minerals frame our bones. Our species survives by the same organic power and complexity that enables eagles to fly and whales to sing.

Knowing who you are as a living being begins with recognizing two apparently opposite truths at one and the same time. The book of Genesis puts both these truths in poetic, prescientific language. "You are dust," Yahweh says to the first man in the primordial garden, "and to dust you shall return" (Genesis 3:19). But when Yahweh formed this man from dust and water, Genesis also says that "He breathed into his nostrils breath of life, and the man became a living soul" (Genesis 2:6-7). Dust we are, but dust that has been watered, shaped, and animated by a power larger than any that is known from human experience.

Genesis understands humanity as a torn condition, limitation paired with an inkling of immortality. Knowing that we are limited comes *with* the awareness of a force deeper, stronger, and more enduring than we can aspire to be.

Contradictions are not easy to live with.

Holding in balance the two truths of the Soul, its limitation and its sense of immortality, is among the greatest challenges a human being can face. It is easy, and a frequent human failing, to try to pass oneself off as more powerful than is truly the case, to evade the truth of limitation. From the worst tyrants of human history to the petty bullies who have ruined the lives of countless families, the drive to pretend to more control than one can really exert is typically and tragically human.

Equally typical is the opposite response: the despair that expects nothing but the short life one has been allotted until the inevitable death comes. This advice is explored in the book of Ecclesiastes, one of the most challenging works in the Bible, "I have seen all the works done under the sun, and look—all are vanity and chasing after wind" (Ecclesiastes 1:14). A similar attitude is expressed by Jean-Paul Sartre, the twentieth-century Existentialist: "When you live alone you no longer know what it is to tell something: the plausible disappears at the same time as the friends. You let events flow past; suddenly you see people pop up who speak and who go away, you plunge into stories without beginning or end."[1]

Both the desire to dominate events and bleak despair arise in the emotional lives of many people and are woven into the events of human history. If human capacities were infinite, domination might seem plausible; even then, what would happen when two infinitely capable human beings disagreed with one another? If all we had to say about life, on the other hand, is that it is difficult and then ends, then despair would have to be recommended.

Western philosophers have made careers out of attempting to reduce the ambivalence of the human Soul to one alternative or the other. Between Friedrich Nietzsche's ideal of the superman and Sartre's recommendation of living with a sense of emptiness, there seems little to choose. But other thinkers, especially from the ancient world, have understood that the Soul is ambivalent by its nature. Authentic wisdom involves coming to terms with both human mortality and the human aspiration to eternity.

The term "soul" in Hebrew (*nephesh*) can also be translated as "breath" or "life" or "self," depending upon the context involved. The word takes its root, as do the analogous terms in other ancient languages, in the fact that we breathe. In the myth of Genesis, Yahweh infuses breath into Adam's being. People instinctively know that breathing is an absolute requirement of their lives, yet what we breathe in and breathe out is both inside us and outside us, beyond our control. The very act of breathing is both an unconscious and a conscious action, a response that volition can only partially control.

The dichotomy of the Soul, as both a limited identity and yet brushing up against what is eternal, is like the paradox of breath, which involves a small sack of air in a sea of comparatively limitless atmosphere. No wonder human beings, who are capable of self-awareness, desire logical answers to the question of who they are. How can we be finite while we have a sense of what is infinite and eternal?

Sometimes people attempt to choose either limitation within the world or superiority over the world as the true root of the complexity of their lives. Logic naturally wants to reduce events and problems to simple causes. Yet sometimes simplicity distorts more than it explains, and experience shows that seeing people on only one side of the dichotomy between limitation and eternity is a deceptive distortion. To be human includes living with the paradox of being both limited and transcendent, unpredictably vulnerable and strong at one and the same time.

Perhaps the greatest sage of the human Soul was Lao Tsu, a sixth-century B.C.E. Chinese mystic who taught of what he called the "Tao," or the path of life. He said:

> The universe is everlasting.
> The reason the universe is everlasting
> Is that it does not live for Self.
> Therefore it can long endure.
> Therefore the Sage puts himself last,
> And finds himself in the foremost place;
> Regards his body as accidental,
> And his body is thereby preserved.
> Is it not because he does not live for Self
> That his Self is realized?[2]

In this case as in many others, the genius of Lao Tsu lies not in his inventiveness but in his capacity to distill the wisdom of many centuries and cultures into a single, clear insight. What he says represents the wisdom of the ancient world in aggregate. Although the specific view of the Soul or self varied from culture to culture (and within each culture), the wonderful fragility of human being in its pilgrimage toward eternity remains a staple of ancient religious inheritance.

Jesus knew about this primordial inheritance principally through the Judaism of his own culture. But his native Galilee was also shaped by powerful influences outside of Judaism. The Roman occupation of Galilee, begun during the first century B.C.E., brought Greco-Roman culture to Jesus' world. Centuries before that, conquest by the imperial powers of the Assyrians, the Babylonians, and the successors of Alexander the Great, as well as trade with cities as far away as India and China, made Galilee a crucible of religious ideas. At the same time Galilean Jews resorted to their Judaic inheritance—in oral form, since they were illiterate for the most part—in order to withstand absorption by Rome.

In his thinking about the Soul, *naphsha'* in the Galilean Aramaic of his period, Jesus assumed the inherited wealth of ancient religious wisdom. At no point does he offer a basic definition of what *naphsha'* is, because his disciples already understood that. We need to know what they knew about the Soul to appreciate Jesus' teaching.

Jesus presented his own, acute version of the wisdom of Lao Tsu, insisting on the power of selflessness. His teaching grew darker over time, as conflict with the political authorities in Jerusalem became acute and he realized that death at the hands of the Romans might come to him in the shameful, degrading form of crucifixion. But Jesus' words signal to his followers that even the most disgraceful of executions can open the way of life (Mark 8:34, translated from the Greek text): "If anyone wants to come after me, deny himself and take his cross and follow me!"

After this challenging call, Mark's Gospel has Jesus add that "Whoever wishes to save his own life, will ruin it, but whoever will ruin his life for me and the message will save it" (Mark 8:35). That puts the same underlying wisdom in more general, abstract terms. The Gospels often use repetition and paraphrase to convey Jesus' difficult teachings. In the case of these two sayings, a single truth, that the self needs to be lost for the self to be gained, is expressed as an imperative, to take up the cross, and as a proverb, about how to save one's life. These are teachings designed for meditation and careful incorporation into life, not just for quick learning or routine acceptance. Those who put Mark's Gospel together from oral sources show us that they appreciated Jesus was speaking on the basis of common ancient wisdom, such as Lao Tsu also articulated, with a deep engagement with the quest to discover the true resources of the Soul.

Both Jesus and Lao-Tsu vehemently challenged the way many people through the ages have preferred to see their Souls. It would be an enormous consolation if, in the midst of all the changes and anxiety and pain of this life, each of us could think of having within us a spark of eternity, a changeless nucleus of ourselves that no power on earth could take away. From time to time during its history, especially during the Middle Ages, that was how Christianity presented the human Soul, enabling poets such as Dante to describe the journey of men's Souls in either hell or heaven, depending upon their deeds. In either case, Dante portrayed the Soul as an indelible possession.

Dante, together with other medieval thinkers, showed the influence more of Stoic philosophy than the Christian religion. Stoics from Emperor Marcus Aurelius (during the second century) to Boethius (during the sixth century) conceived of the Soul as a vital spark, a calm within the storm of life in which a wise man could seek refuge. The idea of the Soul as inherently immortal remains current today and derives from our primeval past, just as the apprehension of the Soul's fragility does.

Between those two alternatives, however, both Lao-Tsu and Jesus came down on the side of the Soul's fragility, its inherent transience. Lao-Tsu spoke as a philosopher, Jesus as a prophet. But that difference between them in no way implies that Jesus was not coherent in his message about the human Soul. Rather, with great variety of metaphor and wording, he hammered home a persistent message: the Soul was destined to be lost; only radical means could rescue it.

Jesus' challenge comes across in several of his most vivid and memorable statements, about the first being last and the last being first,[3] about his purpose and the purpose of any disciple—to serve rather than to be served,[4] about becoming child in order to convey the power and presence of God.[5] Each of these principles is repeated, tailored to suit its particular position in the Gospel and the passage in which it appears. The ability to bring his grounding themes to bear in a variety of circumstances, but always in ways that insisted on our common humanity, constituted a profound and persistent element of Jesus' teaching.

Jesus did not teach a message of unrelieved pain, or of self-denial for its own sake. The fact of the Soul's fragility could become the gateway to breakthrough, as he says in the Gospel according to John (12:24):

> Unless a germ of wheat has fallen to the ground and died, it
>   remains alone.
> But if it dies, it bears much fruit.

John's presentation sums up the same principle that comes to expression in the earlier Gospels in varying ways.

Sometimes in Christian history, Jesus' teaching—clear and repeated though it is—has been ignored by those who say that they have faith in him. There is no reason to suppose that the distortion of his message has been deliberate in every case (although examples of deliberate, self-interested manipulation are all too well known). Men and women of genuine and deep faith can easily confuse the fashions and ideologies of their own communities with the truths that Jesus taught. Jesus himself lived in a cultural margin, without access to the power of Rome or to the privileged status of the priests in the Temple. Precisely because he was powerless, he could see the world without the distorting lens of those whose vision is warped by the self-interested desire to see their values, their way of life, their philosophy, elevated to the level of immutable, divine dogma.

The deviation of medieval Christianity from Jesus' teaching into Stoicism provides one example of that warping influence, but the tale of distortion carries on until our time. *Time* magazine published a cover story[6] about what is known as the Prosperity Gospel, the beliefs that (1) God wants believers to be rich, and in particular that (2) if you give money to God, God will see to it that you will receive more money. *Time* reported that 61 percent of American Christians believe the first statement, and that 31 percent of them believe the second. Numbers of that kind need to be used with caution. People interrupted in the midst of shopping or other activities are not likely to answer a pollster's questions with great care. *Time*'s numbers nonetheless suggest that the Prosperity Gospel has found resonance among Christian believers in the United States.

Preachers of the Prosperity Gospel in *Time*'s report are by and large more likely to be found on television than in pulpits. The economic situation of televangelists is pretty straightforward: because their medium is expensive, they need to raise a great deal of money in order to broadcast. The most effective means to achieve that aim is to exploit their obvious advantage—immediate contact with people who watch television. A television broadcast can easily reach a large viewer base; even a small broadcast area will compete for the attention of more people than can be fit into almost any local church. Televangelists are driven economically to reach widely with the least common denominator of faith, and they have no financial incentive to dig deep into the commitment of their viewers, or to verify the theology they use to win a bigger viewership.

Viewers whose level of commitment is low or marginal in no way harm a televangelist. All he or she needs to do is convince enough people to give sufficient money—directly or by means of advertising—to meet his or her expenses and generate a profit. In fact, insofar as turning on a television set and sending in a donation is easier and cheaper to do than setting out for church each Sunday ready to contribute enough to keep the congregation going, televangelists can exploit a market advantage.

This market advantage among relatively uncommitted viewers can be improved, if the claims of the Prosperity Gospel can convince viewers that by giving money they will earn profits. In effect, each televangelist can conduct a pyramid scheme, in which his or her prosperity advertises the advantage of giving generously to his or her ministry. Provided enough people respond to meet expenses, the operation means greater wealth for him or her. Whatever you think of the theology involved, it should work for the preachers who promote the scheme, and so it has.

The commercial profit offered by the Prosperity Gospel helps explain why televangelists have also invented a Prosperity Jesus, who promises rewards to those who obey him. Sometimes the appeal of this Jesus has to be wrestled out of the Gospels with little care for what they say. Take this example:[7] "Jesus seldom attended funerals. When He did, it was to arrest death and stop the ceremony."

The logic behind this claim is as tortured as it is superficial, relying on the assumption that, except for those few cases when Jesus performed the most memorable of his healings, he never participated in the simple duty of burying the dead, which the Torah of

Moses commands. Worse, proclaiming a Gospel without pain contradicts Jesus' teaching, repeated in the pages of the New Testament, that service is the gateway to life, rather than self-aggrandizement. As a result, Prosperity preachers are easy targets for theologians—or, for that matter, people who read the New Testament carefully—especially when they are renowned for expensive cars, cosmetic surgery, and designer clothing.

The fact that a target is easy, however, does not make it the right target. The appeal of the Prosperity Gospel is rooted, not so much in the skill of its preachers—who rely on standard methods of merchandising—but in the feeling of desperation among many Americans. Most of us at least some of the time already experience life as a burden, plagued by anxieties in regard to how we can make our way in a competitive world or face illness or cope with the uncertainties that come with our complex economic environment. At those times, Jesus' call to take up your cross and follow him just sounds like an additional, painful burden. The Prosperity Gospel falsifies Jesus' teaching, but its bold appeal to what worries many people most means that it is more attractive to them than the more accurate, but less comforting, message that comes from scholars of the New Testament.

Jesus recognized the problem of the human sense of insecurity in his teaching, and understood that anxiety could only get in the way of understanding his message: "Do not worry about your life, what you should eat or what you should drink, or about your body, what you should wear: is not life more than nourishment and the body than clothing?" The term translated "life" here is the very same word we have been occupied with, "Soul" (*psuche* in Greek and *napsha'* in Aramaic). The whole teaching that this saying introduces (Matthew 6:25-34; Luke 12:22-32) turns on the comparison of our lives to the lilies of the field, which Jesus said were more magnificent than the legendary King Solomon, although lilies do not worry or work.

In the case of people whose worry had gotten the better of them, Jesus applied the same prescription he did to his closest disciples. Learn, he said, what your Soul really is, accept that it is fleeting; you will find the peace that comes, not from chasing the illusion of stability in a restless universe, but from joining the movement that unites all things.

The Gospel according to Thomas is not included in the New Testament, yet this second-century collection of Jesus' teaching often distills his message to its essentials: "If they say to you, from where have you come? tell them, We have come from the light, where the light came to be through itself. It stood and it revealed itself through their image. If they say to you, Who are you? say, We are his sons and we are the elect of the living father. If they ask you, What is the sign of the father in you? tell them, it is a movement and a rest" (saying 50).

Finding that rest in movement and under stress, of course, is no easy matter. But according to Jesus' wisdom, it is precisely in the storm of activity that the eye of still strength shows itself. He refused the way of tranquility and endorsed a path of self-denial, or Soul-denial—a denial that makes a person whole.

In the Greek Gospel according to Mark, the term for denying oneself reflects a more complex Aramaic verb (*nacham*), which means to accept comfort by recognizing your weakness. In the best sense, this is what the Christian contemplative tradition calls the consolation of the Soul: not self-satisfaction, but the drawing of strength in acknowledgement of personal vulnerability. Put back into its original Aramaic, Jesus' teaching in Mark 8:34 is all the stronger in its rhythm and power (with accents here marked with "/"):

> 'In man detsa/bah mey'teyh/ batray/,
> yitnach/am viynsey'/ yat tseliyv/eyh
> veyeyteh/ batray/!
> *If anyone wants to come after me,*
> *He will console himself and take up his cross*
> *come after me!*

The human Soul is built for movement and travel, a constant stretch beyond easy comfort.

I once had what proved to be the good fortune of injuring my back. My physician at the time recognized the injury was serious; I could not run at all, swim, or even walk normally; the constant pain seemed to spread daily. My good fortune came in his treatment, because my body taught me something about my Soul.

One reason I had stayed with my physician was that he was not quick to prescribe medication, even when his patients asked him for drugs. I have to admit, my pain was bad enough that I inquired about medicines that might be available. But my doctor felt that physiotherapy was a better route for me. That proved a transforming experience.

The pain from my neck into my shoulder and upper arm was nagging, if bearable, but any movement of my arm through an arc of more than around 45 degrees became excruciating. Imagine my apprehension, then, when the physiotherapist bent my arm at the elbow, and lifted my upper arm right behind my head. Somehow, she put me into that position almost painlessly. From that posture, she then pushed my arm up from the elbow, in order to exert pressure on my shoulder and work that juncture of bone and muscle and ligament.

The therapist worked with steady strength, engaging me in conversation, and asking me how much pain I felt, and when the pain became sharp. Once she had defined an arc of movement I could bear, which was already greater than my usual 45 degrees, she methodically counted to twenty as she extended the arc further, and returned to my comfort zone again. By the third group of twenty, my shoulder moved almost normally. How was that possible?

As the physiotherapist explained my body to me, the anticipation of physical pain had been producing pain in my shoulder. Whenever I approached the challenge of moving beyond my limited range, the sensation of pain—as a measure of protection—prevented the movement. The therapist showed, however, that my body could unlearn the same pain it had tutored itself to feel.

A great deal of uncertainty surrounds why our bodies feel pain when they do, but the reality of persistent pain without apparent organic cause has been well documented. Physiotherapy itself remains a controversial option. In my case, it was a complete success, when coupled with a program of increased exercise. My medical insurance company, however, wound up removing my doctor from its list of accepted practitioners, because its experts preferred the option of treatment by medication, rather than physiotherapy. The facts that I had cost the company less than I would have by pursuing drug therapy, and that I was able once again to live and work and walk normally, somehow never entered into its thinking.

Pain comes and goes, however we explain it. Sometimes, the causes are truly organic, even when we are not in a position to detect them. But pain is also a learned response, and I found out it is possible, pleasurable, and personally fulfilling to set about unlearning that response. The basic physical strategy of avoiding pain that keeps us out of genuinely dangerous situations can also become debilitating, when immobility makes us literally afraid to move.

That wisdom about my physical body also applies to my Soul. Perhaps even more than in our physical relations with the world and other people, when emotions are involved, caution to the point of fear frequently gets in the way. Many of the attitudes that a person displays in society do not reflect his or her feelings as much as his or her defenses. One person might enter a full room and dominate it with funny stories or political comments, while another sits on the margins, looking for the first opportunity of making a decent escape, and yet another sticks to exchanging a few words only with people he or she already knows. These strategies of getting through a party, with variations and sometimes combinations of differing modes of interaction, are easily observed, and can be an entertaining way to get someone who takes pleasure in observation through the same party with some enjoyment.

These masks of interaction—the garrulous talker, the withdrawn avoider, the conventional conversationalist, and the abstracted observer—have their uses, but they also can become traps, preventing genuine exchanges with other people. At the very least, to become genuine we need to be willing to switch masks, but a better aim—for the sake of Soul, as we will see—is to put all masks aside, and permit who we are to emerge directly from our actions and attitudes.

The Soul is the seat of our intentional actions, the place from which we move out to meet the world. If the Soul is no more than a mask, a pattern of repeated routines that we deploy pretty much no matter what company we find ourselves in, we will never reveal who we are, and our world will be no different for our presence within it. In the end, who we are and what we do are not two different issues but belong to a single continuum.

People have often asked me whether it is more important to concentrate on the work that we do for others or on how we stand in relation to God. Answering that question is a bit tricky, because neither ethical action nor our relationship to God can be described as unimportant. But however I respond to a specific questioner, my aim is always the same: to show that when we act, that is nothing other than a manifestation of ourselves. Ethical action depends upon the capacity of a person to bring his or her personal insight and feeling into the world of social relations. Likewise, the Soul's identity is incomplete, and often entirely unknown, unless it expresses itself in relation to others.

The necessary interface between ethical action and the integrity of our Souls explains why we must interact in order to be who we are, and why only those actions we bring ourselves to fully are genuinely ethical. Although in one sense, as relates to our physical constitution, we are earth, the essence of our Soul's constitution is action. We are made to be on the move, to transcend and extend our concerns beyond ourselves, beyond the last year, the last day, the last moment of our lives.

We are restless, St. Augustine wrote in his *Confessions*,[8] until we find our rest in God. But that rest is dynamic, the movement and rest of which *The Gospel according to Thomas* speaks. Only movement can satisfy our Souls. Our thirst is for transcendence, a way forward that continues who we genuinely are, but at the same time extends what we do and how we feel, providing us with the security that comes, not from the false promise that our material conditions will always be favorable, but from the strength of knowing who we are.

The wisdom that the Soul is more a process than it is an unchanging substance has entered our proverbial wisdom. "Get over yourself" has entered the American idiom somewhere between a friendly reality check and an insult, but the phrase carries an important message. Every person is only as good as his or her ability to step beyond routine interests and goals, and to enter into deliberate action so as to change and improve the world and those around us.

Each of us begins life with the first breath we draw and continues only as long as breathing goes on. Physically, that pattern also expresses who we are at base. We need to release and push out the same air we needed just a breath before in order to survive. That self-emptying in our chest, exaggerated when we are under physical stress, brings a moment of especial vulnerability, as the movement of air outward becomes a gasp to another breath taken in.

The practice of yoga has long concentrated on this simple truth of the Soul, as a movement, a rest, a pulse inward and outward with moments of vulnerability as well as strength. Focused attention on the act of breathing itself often features as the start of a yogic session. The purpose is to raise awareness of breathing itself, but also of the dependence of one's entire body and breathing on the mysterious, vulnerable process of inhaling and releasing.

The fact that Mahatma Gandhi, one of the most successful activists of the twentieth century, practiced and commended the practice of disciplined breathing is no coincidence. He wrote in 1945, for example:

> Deep breathing is essential. Close one nostril and breathe deeply through the other. You can gradually increase it to half an hour.

Utter Ramanama with every breath you take. When doing breathing exercises, you should have fresh air on all sides. It would be better to do it in the open. You should do it every morning without fail and afterwards at least four times after the food has been digested. Breathe in and breathe out. This exercise should be taken slowly.[9]

Gandhi took his own advice, and his policy of nonviolence, inextricably connected with his religious practice, proved successful in enabling India to shed its colonial status and become an independent nation.

"Nonviolence," a translation of the Sanskrit term *ahimsa*, names a strategy of engagement for change that rejects violent force, while discovering other resources of transformation. As Gandhi said, "Nonviolence is impossible without humility,"[10] an accurate sense of who one is and is not. The brilliance of the approach is that it uses human vulnerability, usually perceived as a matter of weakness, as a strong pivot of moral change. Peaceful protest in the face of armed troops, fasting in order to mourn injustice, silent resistance to evil, and—when necessary—submission to arrogance in a way that makes plain how immoral it is, are all included under the category of nonviolence.

Nonviolence is not merely the absence of violence. More precisely, it is the vulnerability to turn the other cheek, as Jesus said, when one is struck (Matthew 5:39). Jesus' teaching in this regard came into full focus during his last months in Jerusalem, although it has deep roots in his experience before that time. By uncovering those circumstances, we can appreciate the power of his ethics. Despite his lack of precise information concerning the politics of Rome, and therefore the growing personal threat to him of Pontius Pilate, Jesus knew that he courted danger during this period.

The constant threat of violence took a toll on his followers, as Jesus well knew. They literally had to be ready to give up wealth and family, to ruin their lives if necessary, for the sake of discipleship. The message that God's Kingdom was to be all consuming, dissolving even Caesar's power, made it tolerable to bear the Romans' cross if necessary. God will one day be all in all, and his Kingdom alone will stand; it is worth giving everything to realize the Kingdom's fullness. Jesus speaks of doing that when he refers to his followers as a whole, not only his own fate. Everyone needs to find the cross and take it up on the way that leads to God's Kingdom.

Both Jesus (who taught publicly between the death of John the Baptist in 21 C.E. and his own death in 32 C.E)[11] and Matthew (written in Damascus c. 80 C.E.) understood the threat of Roman soldiers, who were authorized to take what they needed from pilgrims and force them into labor. The teaching about turning the other cheek represented in Matthew 5:38-48 is not, as commonly supposed, a timeless adage against resistance to any and all injustice but a strategy of coping with soldiers who took what they needed, by violence if necessary. In the face of the Roman Empire's evil, retaliate with the good that provides by example the prospect that justice might prevail, as well a chance of avoiding harm.

Some popular theologians have persistently taken this teaching out of its original social context and made Jesus into a philosopher of blanket nonresistance. But his powerful wisdom speaks from the conditions that he and the Matthean community faced. Mahatma Gandhi and Martin Luther King, Jr., rightly saw that Jesus did not teach acquiescence to evil but an exemplary retaliation that shows evil up for what it truly is.

Jesus was a source of Gandhi's teaching, and Gandhi was a source of Martin Luther King, Jr.'s teaching, but the inherent wisdom of their positions goes beyond any single culture or time. Finally, all three of them looked into the reality of the human Soul and found that vulnerability was not weakness but a message from one Soul to another of the necessity of justice.

Jesus' insistence that his disciples needed to be prepared to lose their Souls in order to gain them finds elucidation in a haunting scene in the Gospels. Mark, the earliest of the Gospels, sets out the scene the most vividly of them all (Mark 14:32-43):

> And they come to a tract whose name was Gethsemane, and he says to his students, "Sit here while I pray." And he takes along Peter and James and John with him, and he began to be completely bewildered and distressed, and he says to them, "My soul is mournful unto death: remain here and be alert." He went before a little and fell upon the ground and was praying so that, if it were possible, the hour might pass on from him. And he was saying, "Abba, Father: all things are possible for you. Carry this cup on, away from me! Yet not what I want, but what you!" And he comes and finds them sleeping, and says to Peter, "Simon, are you sleeping? You were not capable of being alert one hour? Be alert and pray, so that you do not come into a test. The Spirit is willing, but the flesh is weak." He again went away and prayed. Having said the same thing, he again came and found them sleeping, because their eyes were weighed down; and they did not know what to reply to him. And he comes the third time and says to them, "Sleep for what remains and repose: it suffices. The hour has come, Look: the son of man is delivered up into the hands of sinners. Be raised, we go. Look: the one who delivers me over has approached." And at once while he is still speaking Judas, one of

the Twelve, comes along, and with him a crowd with swords and clubs from the high priests and the scribes and the elders.

This scene, first written in Mark's crabbed, inelegant Greek (which I have put into the closest correspondence to English possible) achieves its power by what it says about Jesus, and by how it weaves his experience of human weakness into the experience of his followers.

Jesus openly admits his weakness, his "soul is mournful unto death," and he wants his disciples near to comfort him. His words are not just a general admission of grief; rather, he speaks in the words of Jonah at Nineveh (Jonah 4:9), another case of a prophet who sorrowed at the vocation given him by God. That is what makes Jesus' anguish at this moment arresting from the outset. Although depicted from the beginning of Mark's Gospel as God's Son, here Jesus is not even sure he can complete his work as a prophet.

Jesus asks for the "hour" to pass him by—and to leave him alive. The term "hour" in Mark's Gospel refers both to his personal fate (the time of his death), and to the moment when everything he has done will reach its climax in the disclosure of God's Kingdom. How can God's Son be praying to elude that climactic realization of what he has done and who he has always been? An ancient critic of Christianity, the second-century classicist Celsus,[12] picked up on the scene in Gethsemane, asking how Jesus could possibly "mourn and lament and pray to escape the fear of death." The contrast in Celsus's mind was between Jesus and philosophical heroes such as Socrates, who faced their deaths with a noble, Stoic calm.

Had Celsus known the Gospels better, he could have sharpened his criticism—and he no doubt would have done so. When Jesus asks for "this cup" to be taken from him, that reflects the Aramaic idiom, the "cup of death." Yet in Mark he has been predicting his death, speaking of its necessity with greater and greater specificity, and explaining to his followers that they had to be prepared to take this same path (Mark 8:31-38; 9:30-37; 10:32-45). He has already said that they would drink the cup that he drinks (10:39) and that his purpose was to give his life for redemption (10:45). His hesitation now, unless it has some deeper purpose, seems not only a matter of cringing in the face of pain and death but also of denying his divine mission and misleading his disciples. This passage represents a searching challenge to the belief that suffering is necessary, and the way this challenge is posed is key to the whole Gospel's meaning.

This section of Mark belongs to one of the earliest oral sources in all the Gospels—the account of Jesus' passion and death crafted by Peter and his companions. Prayer featured vitally in this oral proto-Gospel, and Peter stressed the importance of intense repetition in prayer. In Gethsemane, Jesus brings his anguish to his *Abba* three times. Peter's source spoke of Jesus' prayer, not merely to give information about Jesus, but in order to model for believers how they themselves should pray when in distress.

The desire to model how believers should confront the challenge of suffering helps explain why liturgical rhythms and antiphonal exchanges of dialogue ripple through the story of Gethsemane. It is designed as part of Peter's passion narrative, the story of Jesus' suffering up to and including the moment of his death. Those events were particularly commemorated and recited by Christians every year prior to Easter, the Sunday of the resurrection, the Sunday when converts were baptized after extensive preparation by means of study, vigils of prayer during the night, and fasting. Those converts joined Jesus liturgically in Gethsemane, and searched themselves to see whether they were ready for the "hour"—the decisive moment of potential danger and revelation—that their baptism represented.

In Peter's passion narrative, there was a human failing to be avoided prior to moments of decision. But that failing was not the impulse to plead for one's life: that is just what Jesus does, three times over, and without earning blame from Peter's story or from God. The obstacle to be overcome is rather the languor that came to the disciples during their vigil with Jesus (Mark 14:37-38). Love of life is no fault; dozy adherence to convention is what gets in the disciples' way. By contrast, Peter's story *commends and endorses* Jesus' open expression of fear and doubt. This is prayer as it should be—directed to God as one's *Abba*, which in Aramaic means both "father" and "source,"[13] and completely open in its acknowledgment of human weakness.

Peter's understanding, although shaped to suit the needs of liturgy, corresponds well to the historical circumstances that Jesus faced. His campaign against the high priestly administration in the Temple—climaxing in his violent expulsion of animals and their vendors—had put Jesus in danger. But the complexities of power politics eluded him. He could not have known that the execution of Pilate's protector in Rome, Sejanus,[14] would dispose Pilate to put his military resources and might at the disposal of the high priest, Caiaphas.

Even a few weeks prior to Jesus' action in the Temple, an alliance between Pilate and Caiaphas seemed unimaginable. In Gethsemane, the unthinkable became real. The imminent danger of crucifixion—deliberately the most painful and shameful of deaths, which Roman authority alone could command—only became fully apparent to

Jesus when Roman soldiers as well as police from the Temple joined in the attempt to capture him.

In the Gethsemane scene, Peter conveys the moment when Jesus in his mind's eye confronted the might of Rome, not only the anger of the high priest, and asked his God whether such a fate was truly necessary. Peter's portrayal of Jesus' agony of doubt contradicts the conventional view of Jesus as the all-knowing Messiah who is in complete control of his passions.

That conventional view gained traction over time, as one can see by comparing how later Gospels handle the same scene described in Mark. Taking all the accounts in comparison, it is obvious that, as time went on, Christians became less and less comfortable with Jesus being indecisive or fearful in the face of death. Yet whatever their discomfort, the story of Jesus in Gethsemane has remained firmly fixed in the memory of Christians and in the store of accumulated human knowledge concerning how people can learn the ways of God.

The wisdom of Gethsemane acknowledges that, as Jesus approached his death, strong elements of uncertainty remained in his mind. He did not fully appreciate where his own actions in the Temple were taking him and admitted that his Soul was mournful unto death. His vulnerability was not only a strategy but also a tragic fact of his life.

This sense of brokenness within one's being accompanies the lives and the teaching of Gandhi and King, as well. In different ways, both these men became entangled in the twentieth century's characteristic tragic flaw, sexuality.

Time summarized Gandhi's disciplined but strange practice:

> At 36, convinced that sex was the basis of all impulses that must be mastered if man was to reach Truth, he renounced it. An

aspirant to a godly life must observe the Hindu practice of Brahmacharya, or celibacy, as a means of self-control and a way to devote all energy to public service. Gandhi spent years testing his self-discipline by sleeping beside young women. He evidently cared little about any psychological damage to the women involved. He also expected his four sons to be as self-denying as he was. [15]

King's problems were more obvious, and provided the Federal Bureau of Investigation with ample material to accuse him of adultery and to discredit him in the eyes of those with whom the FBI shared its illegally gathered evidence.[16] Neither Gandhi's exaggerated celibacy, nor King's profligacy, can be described as unusual faults. The opposite is the case.

No human hero or sage has ever been perfect. Even those who have explored the depths of the Soul—and perhaps those people in particular—have not escaped the limitation of our nature, a limitation that is not only a matter of our mortality but also of our inability to control entirely what we do.

Jesus told a parable of two sons. One son refused to work in his father's vineyard but then repented and helped; the other said he would help but did nothing (Matthew 21:28-31). In the end this story concerns forgiveness as well as sin. Forgiveness comes from sources outside the Soul, which we will investigate in chapter 5. Yet the Soul itself, as part of its journey into wisdom, needs always to be aware that it is never immune from sin, and that its strength resides, not in any supposed self-sufficiency, but in its capacity to discern its weakness and to correct its direction by following God's will.

Like his contemporaries and the Judaic tradition as a whole, Jesus understood sin as a failure, a missing of one's aim. In fact, the basic verb to "sin"—in Hebrew (*chata'*) as well as in Greek (*hamar-tano*)—means to fail to reach the target, as in archery. The persistence of our missing our purpose is part of our nature. We might be like the son who rebelled and then came around to his father's request, or like the son who seemed cooperative but then did not follow through; but in either case recalcitrance is inherent in our Souls.

The Soul, the seat of the self, needs to emerge—like Jesus in Gethsemane—in its vulnerabilities as well as its strengths, in its commitments as well as its recalcitrance, in its pulse defined by our breathing, in order to serve as the source of purposeful action. In acting, however, it also needs to be aware of the weight of its sin. Turned into itself alone, a Soul will inevitably lose its sense of purpose and indulge its self-regard. Made for movement and travel, standing still is its one fatal flaw. The Soul's sensitivity to other powers, outside itself, can alone rescue it from this flaw.

Each of us has a Soul, just as all of us come from the earth. Because the Soul is who we are, we might think we know our inmost selves. But that is not our common experience. Experience shows that people often ignore their strengths as well as their weaknesses, and that who they say they are—even to themselves—is more like a mask than like an honest estimate of their shortcomings, aspirations, and resources.

Souls are made for the company of others, just as they are meant for movement and purposeful activity. Like breathing, the action from which the word for Soul arose, Souls are designed to sustain life, and vigorous exercise improves their operation. Breath comes with difficulty to people who do not exercise, yet practice makes their breathing and their heart-function and their muscles and their movements more enjoyable and efficient. Those who wonder about their Souls can ask themselves whether they are using them enough.

Just as a certain aerobic level is necessary to improve the fitness of bodies, so Souls require a certain amount of social activity to achieve and maintain their health. People out of touch with their Souls will not fulfill the prophetic vocation of repairing and renewing the world. We are in need of communities where we can know we are accepted as who we are, where we enter into purposeful actions we believe in, and where our interactions with others will both encourage our strengths and correct our flaws.

Fortunately, communities of this kind are near to hand. Not only churches and mosques and synagogues, but also voluntary organizations, investment clubs, rifle associations, political parties, and support groups have long belonged to the fabric of our societies. Taken together, they mean that virtually every person may find a place of his or her Soul's community.

Of course, belonging to a community does not mean, by itself, that you will change the world. But the opportunity to know and to develop your Soul might well point you in the direction of prophetic change. When I first arrived in the church that I serve, a woman who called herself Fritzi was a mainstay of what we did. She organized, baked, cleaned, ironed, and folded linen, visited people in the congregation, and on special occasions made a wonderful meatloaf, all of that apart from volunteering at our local hospital. Each interaction would produce from her some remark or reflection, a joke or a reminder or a little rebuke, that left whoever she dealt with a little the wiser and a bit more thoughtful than he or she had been before. I wondered what had made Fritzi so vital.

Thirty years before I met her, Fritzi was diagnosed with cancer of the stomach. Her survival was unusual. So was her reaction to survival. She decided that both the church and the hospital, the institutions that had brought her through her illness, deserved her help; and she never wavered in her devotion. At the time she started supporting those institutions, both of them were marginal, the hospital near to a merger and the church about to close. Today both of them are thriving, independent concerns, and many people at each place still have a story to tell you about Fritzi, her gravelly voice, and how she made them feel welcome and safe. As far as I know, the biggest regret in her life was that she had once made her daughter stand in a corner too long. Her daughter had no memory of that incident.

One morning Fritzi's sister called me in some concern, because Fritzi did not answer her telephone. We both went to her apartment and found that Fritzi had died in her sleep. She was in bed, with a book and glass of sherry near to hand. A friend remarked to me, "She died the death of a saint." I thought to myself that perhaps that was because she had lived the life of a saint. Fritzi was my sage when it concerns how to live with an awareness of one's Soul.

2
Spirit

"Spirit" might seem practically synonymous with "Soul," the way those two words are often used. Both terms sometimes refer in common speech to the eternal aspect of a person, the human element that gives hope for life after death. There is an overlap between Spirit and Soul that we have to make sense of in this chapter. But first of all, we need to disentangle the two words, starting at the Bible's beginning in order to understand the ways of Spirit.

The Hebrew Bible begins its story with the primeval narrative of the book of Genesis, which evokes the power of God's Spirit within the world. The epic of Genesis speaks of the origins of the world, when divine Spirit alone could bring life out of chaotic darkness. But Genesis also conceives of creation as a continuing process. According to the ancient Israelite conception, Spirit exerts her influence incessantly, holding the world in being and revealing the true substance of that world to people.

When speaking of Spirit, I deliberately say "her influence," rather than "its influence" or "his influence." "Spirit," the noun *ruach* in Hebrew, is feminine in gender, and that femininity is more than a matter of grammar in the Hebrew Bible. Sometimes Spirit is personified as a woman precisely when her creative power is at issue. The opening chapter of Genesis, which forms the charter for understanding the Spirit in the biblical tradition, is the object of meditation in the book of Proverbs, where "Spirit" (*ruach*) is further identified with "Wisdom" (*chokhmah*), another feminine noun. When Wisdom speaks in Proverbs, she articulates Spirit's relationship to God and to humanity in a way that reverberates through all the Abrahamic traditions.

Proverbs' presentation helps us see how ancient Israelites understood God's Spirit, at the same time that it provides readers of all epochs, ancient and modern, with clues for understanding the basic concept of divine creation expressed in Genesis. Within the biblical tradition and all the interpretations that tradition has fed, Spirit has combined the themes of God's creative power and humanity's ability to internalize that power.

In the passage from Proverbs (8:22-31) the speaker is Wisdom— Spirit herself:

> Yahweh possessed me in the beginning of his way,
>> Before his works of old.
> From everlasting I was established,
>> From the beginning, before the earth...
> When he established the heavens, I was there,
>> When he drew a circle on the face of the deep.
> When he made firm the skies above,
>> When the fountains of the deep grew strong,
> When he placed the boundary of the sea,
>> And waters did not transgress his command,
> When he marked the foundations of the earth,
> I was beside him as an architect, and I was daily his delight,
>> Pleasuring him in every time,
> Pleasuring the expanse of the earth,
>> and my delight was with the sons of men.

The elegant poetry of Proverbs follows the thought of Genesis, as well as its logical structure and vivid imagery.

In Genesis, God's creative acts come from the divine Spirit, which "hovered over the face of the waters" (Genesis 1:1). The imagery evokes a picture of primeval chaos, the whole conceivable universe awash in primordial waters that could not be managed and did not yet sustain any form of life. God's Spirit, a term that in Hebrew can also mean "wind," pushed aside the chaotic, fluid mass and shaped the possibilities, the forces, and the basic structures of life.

The word "hovered" in Genesis 1:1 conjures up the image of a bird, in the case of Spirit invisible and powerful, whose force is felt only by the draft of her mighty wings. In the strong but gentle rhythm of the Bible's first chapter, light and dark, heaven and earth, plants and planets, fish and fowl, animals and man all flow from the power of Spirit. God creates the last creature, humanity, in the divine image and likeness—as Genesis 1:26-27 specifies— both male and female. The power of that statement, which comes as God is completing the physical structure of creation, is that it speaks divine nature as well as human nature. Genesis presents all humanity as equally in God's image, whether males or females are at issue, and at the same time embeds this equal balance of sexuality within God's image and likeness.

The shaping power that brings about an affinity of nature between God and humanity, according to Genesis, is Spirit. Soul is the form of life proper to people as people, but Spirit shapes and provides that form. In addition, their creation in the divine image and likeness means that human beings also have access to understanding God's Spirit. Fashioned by the power of Spirit so that their identity—their very Soul—bears the stamp of the divine, humanity is in the unique position to sense and understand the power of Spirit, the primordial *and* ambient reality of God in the world.

Proverbs 8 explores just this connection between the Spirit and humanity, teasing out what it means for the Spirit to shape life and for humanity to comprehend the Spirit. Wisdom is presented as the inner, sensible content of Spirit, the interior purpose of the force of wind. She is portrayed as the designer or architect who frames life, as Proverbs crafts another way of looking at God's creation when the Spirit of God hovered over the waters.

Wisdom also discloses God to humans, by the delight they can take in perceiving the order of the world's expanse, a delight made possible by being created in the divine image and likeness. Even as she stood by God as his counselor, Wisdom was "pleasuring the expanse of the earth, and my delight was with the sons of men." This is where the gender of Spirit or Wisdom, and her personification as a woman, involves a vital principle within the Hebrew Bible. Just as male and female are in the image of God, so also God is conceived of as possessing both male and female attributes. This means that the act of creation was a delight, as Wisdom declares that she was "daily his delight" in Proverbs. With this same capacity to engender delight, Wisdom opens up the curiosity and enjoyment of beauty among human beings.

Some interpreters have rightly observed that this whole alternation of genders, from God's masculinity to the Spirit's femininity and then to the supposed masculinity of male sages in Israel, presupposes a model of male dominance. That is obviously the case: by the time the Hebrew Bible came to be written, male dominance—an inheritance of the emergence of cities during the Stone Age that were constantly preoccupied with war and committed to the male hierarchy of armies—had been ensconced for thousands of years.[1]

But it would be naïve to expect the Bible, or any document, not to be influenced by its ambient culture. From the divine mandate that male Israelite soldiers should utterly exterminate their enemies, including all living things in Jericho, in an act of destruction called *cherem* (Joshua 6:16-26) to God's promise to David that one of his sons would always sit on the throne of Israel (2 Samuel 7:12-16), male dominance is an unmistakable part of the Hebrew Bible.

The dominance of masculine vocabulary and conception became even more extreme in the later history of Christianity. By the fourth century C.E., theologians who discussed the Trinity commonly referred to the Spirit as a man, alongside the Father and the Son. That change was aided by shifts in language, because "Spirit" is in the neuter gender in Greek (*pneuma*), while it is masculine in Latin (*spiritus*). As compared to the male exclusivity in thinking about God in Christianity after Constantine, male dominance in the Israelite conception appears almost benign.

The conceptions of Spirit in both Genesis and Proverbs not only offer a less egregious form of male dominance than elsewhere in Judaism and Christianity. More profoundly, both biblical books also develop conceptions of gender that are complementary.

In Genesis, it is Spirit who begins the creation by her hovering over the face of the primeval waters (Genesis 1:2), and then God speaks in order to create light (Genesis 1:3). The movement of Spirit's power together with divine reason produce the world, and at the close of primordial creation, people are made both male and female in the divine image and likeness (Genesis 1:26-27).

Proverbs, on the other hand, goes out of its way to place the initiative of creation with God (Proverbs 8:22), but then makes

Wisdom the primary counselor or architect of divine activity (Proverbs 8:30). By the time of Proverbs, Spirit as Wisdom is more associated with the design of the universe, while Yahweh is identified as the power in creation. That represents a reversal of the roles set out in Genesis, where Spirit is more the power behind events and God more the designer. The point of this reversal was obviously not to produce contradiction, nor is there any wish in Proverbs to replace the conception of Genesis. Rather, Proverbs shows how flexibly ancient Israelites thought about the process of creation as a reflection of the divine nature in its male and female aspects.

In the ancient Israelite conception of divine nature, where female and male are balanced, the principle of the complementarity of the two is more important than the desire to begin with the feminine aspect (as in Genesis 1) or the masculine aspect (as in Proverbs 8). Complementarity is not hierarchy. The whole divine nature might initiate action with one aspect of its being or another, but the aim of its total being is to communicate with people, to relate God's intentions to human beings. For that reason Spirit or Wisdom was a natural part of prophetic vocabulary, as the complement of a male portrayal of God, which made divine purpose more accessible.

Spirit was a central component of Jesus' vision of God, as poetic as the dove he saw descending upon him when he was baptized, as grounded in the earth as the waters of John's baptism, and as powerful as the God who created the universe and liberated Israel from Egypt.

When Jesus spoke of a woman baking as a reflection of God's activity (Luke 13:21) or referred to himself as a mother bird gathering her young (Matthew 23:37), he was not just thinking up arresting images, although they *are* striking and vibrant. The lush fecundity of Wisdom in Jesus' mind was as basic to God as differences of gender were to the people who were created in God's image. On one occasion Jesus even spoke in Wisdom's name, and portrayed himself as her emissary (Luke 11:49), "For this reason also the Wisdom of God said, I myself will delegate to them prophets and agents."

Wisdom was a source of revelation, part of the divine image and likeness. For that reason, Wisdom could also be embodied in each female disciple, and Jesus' relationships with his female disciples did not have to be sexually intimate for him to devote himself to the persistent, cherishing care that a lover devotes to the beloved. He saw the relationship between masculine and feminine as part of the power of God, inherent in the connection between the Spirit and the Father of all.

The insight of Genesis, like the insight of Proverbs, claims that human beings can understand the Spirit, both in the sense of the creative power of God, which Genesis stresses, and the wise intelligence of God, which Proverbs emphasizes. Naturally, any claim of the affinity of divine Spirit with people implies their close relationship with God, simply because they are human beings. But an awareness of that connection comes as a special gift, as the story of Jesus' baptism in the Gospels makes plain.

Ancient Israelite cosmology echoes in the scene of Jesus' baptism. Water and wind since the time of Genesis have symbolized Spirit as the animating aspect of God, his infinite capacity to generate new forms of life. Jesus believed in the classic Israelite perspective that all creation was infused with the pulse of God, "he looks on the earth and it trembles; he touches the mountains and they smoke" (Psalm 104:32). God's creative power was not only primordial, something unleashed before time could be reckoned;

Spirit *was* active then, of course, but she was also happening every day, moment by moment.

When God turned his face away or withheld his Spirit, his creatures perished and crumbled to dust, while that same Spirit constantly renewed life (Psalm 104:29-30). God was capable at any time of destroying the world and creating new heavens and a new earth (Isaiah 65:17), and yet as Jesus himself said, all living things, the simplest birds, find their sustenance in God (Matthew 6:26; Luke 12:24).

Jesus' especial devotion to the reality of Spirit in the world was grounded in his youthful association with John the Baptist. John taught his own characteristic kind of "immersion," which is what the word *baptisma* means in Greek (rendering the Aramaic term *tebiyla'*). Immersion in water was a basic religious practice in Judaism, as in ancient religions generally.

Water was commonly held to renew and purify, to prepare a person for fellowship with God in worship or with fellow human beings, if impurity or sin had caused a person to be isolated from the community. To John, however, that view of immersion or baptism did not go far enough. The true function of baptism, in his teaching, was to ready a person to receive forgiveness and the Spirit of God.

John the Baptist and all his disciples built up the expectation that God's Spirit was ready to be poured out on Israel anew, as it had been at the time of Moses, when God liberated his people from slavery, gave them the Torah, and led them into the promised land. That caused many people to see first John, and then Jesus, as a prophet who was inspired (literally "breathed into") by Spirit and who could speak directly on God's behalf. Prophecy in the Hebrew Bible often begins with the words, "Thus says the LORD." The introduction is no mere figure of speech. It is a claim on the part of the prophets who speak these words to pronounce the will and the mind of God.

For ancient rabbis like John and Jesus, Spirit animated life, held each particle of the universe in place, and set it spinning on command. Encoded in that same animating force was God's omnipotent intelligence, his plan for the world, in short: Wisdom herself. Spirit was revealed in Israel's history; and Israel's prophets, when the Spirit was upon them, were able to speak with God's voice.

Jesus' repetitive, committed practice, and his sometimes inadequate diet and exposure to the elements contributed to the intensity of his vision of God's presence. Under John's tutelage, he altered his consciousness and entered the world of the Spirit. As he immersed for purification, a repeated practice among John the Baptist's followers, not the once-for-all baptism of later ritual, Jesus came to have an increasingly vivid vision. He saw the heavens *splitting* open and God's Spirit descending upon him as a dove. And he heard a voice: "you are my son, the beloved; in you I take pleasure" (Matthew 3:13-17; Mark 1:9-11; Luke 3:21-22).

Simple though this narrative may seem, it conveys Jesus' revelation—grounded in John the Baptist's teaching—that Spirit could and would change the world. Spirit was the link between God's presence and the spread of his powerful influence, his Kingdom on earth. God's Kingdom will take up our attention in the next chapter, but for now we can define it as the power by which God's will can be known and done. Spirit was what effects the Kingdom, bringing it to realization. This is what Jesus saw descend on him through the tear in heaven's veil.

The imagery of the sky opening and a dove descending may appear totally tranquil, but that is *not* in keeping with the sense of cosmological disruption and potential for transformation that the Gospels convey.

In ancient Jewish thought, the heavens were viewed as hard shells above the earth, so that the dove's descent involves breaking open those "firmaments." The term "firmament" comes to us in English from the King James Version of the Bible in Genesis 1:6-8, which correctly translates the original Hebrew (*raqia'*), "God called the firmament Heaven." In view of the association between the firmament and heaven, people commonly think of it as being airy. But the "firmament" of Genesis is literally firm and watertight. It is a *raqia'*, a hammered-out metallic shell.

In this cosmology, the firmament protects the earth, which was seen by the ancient Hebrews as a fragile, disk-shaped bubble surrounded on all sides by an infinite sea. Any break in the bubble's shell is fraught with danger, as when the windows of the heavens were opened at the time of Noah (Genesis 7:11) and the great flood poured down through the firmament and engulfed the earth.

In the conception of ancient Judaism, at any time the bubble could be crushed, not merely punctured, by the forces around it. These forces were not limited to water in Hebrew cosmology. Beyond the firmament, directly over the Temple in Jerusalem, the whole realm of God's unspeakably powerful court was arrayed.

There the prophet Isaiah saw a vision of God's presence in a classic scene of the Bible. Seraphim—not the pink cherubs of Renaissance art, but enormous, burning, multi-winged snakes—thundered in praise of God (Isaiah 6:1-5). Their angelic praise echoes to this day in churches that repeat a version of their words when they celebrate God's presence in the Eucharist (also known as the Mass and the Lord's Supper): "Holy, holy, holy, is the LORD of hosts; the whole earth is full of his glory." In this worship as in the vision of Isaiah, human beings are seen as capable of joining the panoply of angels around God in acknowledging divine reality.

Isaiah's vision concerned only a few of the ten thousand spirits and angels that served the heavenly King, the angelic "hosts," "multitudes," or "armies" who stand at God's behest—a pantheon of fearsome, irresistible might, described for example in the book of Deuteronomy (33:2). God's Spirit—with all its potential to create and destroy—could be revealed by any of these creatures as they descended into the human world.

The monotheism of Judaism and Christianity (and Islam, at a later stage) did not prevent these religions from developing heavenly cosmologies as elaborate as the Olympian court of Zeus. For Jesus, God's Spirit was not just emanation and energy; it went beyond the more philosophical ideas of divine intelligence and voice. It was a force so potent that it could take any shape it liked. For Jesus, the sun and moon were dragged across the firmament by God's Spirit in the form of a host of angels, and at each thin spot in the firmament there was an angel, guarding the potential breach or portal into the pantheon. These thin spots were stars, the divine protection Jesus and other Jews of his time saw when they looked into the sky at night.

When Jesus saw the heavens split open in the midst of his vision, it was a signal for him that, for good or ill, the panoply of spiritual power around God was being released into the world. Yet he saw the Spirit of God, not as a Seraph or an angel of war, but as a dove, hovering over him and descending, as it once had over the primordial waters of creation (Genesis 1:2).

The divine Spirit, creating the new, more human sensibility that Ezekiel had predicted centuries before in Yahweh's name, had come again into the world (Ezekiel 36:25-26):

I will pour upon you pure waters, and you shall be pure; from all
your impurities and from all your idols I will purify you. I will
give you a new heart, and a new spirit I will put in your midst,
and I will remove the heart of stone from your flesh and give you
a heart of flesh.

After the advent of the dove, John and his disciples viewed Jesus
as the beginning of the fulfillment of the prophetic promise of
Israel. In the wilderness of the Jordan, Jesus received from the close
group of visionaries around him the first indication of the special
role he might play in Israel's destiny.

John called Jesus "the lamb of God that takes away the sin of the
world" (John 1:29, 36). That image conveys how John cherished his
young Galilean disciple as a prime student of his teaching. The
lamb symbolized the link between God and humanity, the means
by which the obstacle of sin could be removed by sacrifice so that
people's access to the divine could be restored.

A similar connection came to expression when Jesus heard a
divine voice calling him "Son," a designation that he took to heart.
Contrary to a widespread fallacy, the language of divine sonship is
by no means a Christian invention. The term "son" is used frequently in the Hebrew Bible to denote the intimate relationship
between God and other beings. Messengers before God's throne,
"angels" as we call them in English (from *anggeloi* in Greek;
mal'akhim in Hebrew), are called "Sons of God" (Genesis 6:2). All
Israel is also referred to as a divine Son (Hosea 11:1); and the king
in David's line can be assured by a divine voice, "You are my Son,
this day have I begotten you!" (Psalm 2:7). These are all evidently
expressions, not of a biological relationship, but of the direct revelation that God extends to favored people and angels; they are

indeed "the beloved," as Jesus became as a result of his vision when he immersed, following what John taught.

When Jesus spoke of himself as divine Son, he was not talking in the extravagant, metaphysical language of a later time and theology, which claimed that he had no human father. Rather, he claimed that he stood in the spiritual lineage of Israel's seers, the visionaries who meditated on the divine presence and were blessed with the Spirit that poured out from that source.

Jesus experienced not only the purity of John's immersion but also the seal of divine Spirit, indicating that his purification was complete and genuine, so as to forge a connection between the realms of heaven and earth. John's trust in his young disciple had been rewarded. As far as John and his followers were concerned, Jesus' baptism signaled that the gates of heaven were open again for the Spirit to descend upon Israel, just as John had prophesied.

Was the voice that addressed Jesus really God's, or was it a figment of his prophetic imagination? Deciding one way makes a person inclined to accept Jesus' message as a whole. Deciding that Jesus was sincere, but deluded, obviously implies that he cannot be trusted in all he taught. This decision must remain a matter of personal judgment and is an example of the kinds of assessments that are involved in questions of faith.

Ambiguity belongs to the nature of a prophet's experience: he or she claims access to a level of reality beyond common perception so that acceptance of the claim demands recognition of the prophet's authority. Moses, Jesus, and Muhammad were all at one time or another rejected by the people they sought to serve. Moses came down from Sinai to find his people worshipping a golden calf; Jesus was derided by many respected teachers of his land, threatened with death by the local governor, driven from his native

Galilee, and finally executed in Jerusalem under the authority of Rome; the people of Mecca oppressed Muhammad and then went to war against him after the prophet left that city for Medina.

Long after these and other great seers died, violent divisions have often erupted between people and nations over whether they spoke with God's voice. Even those who have embraced a given prophet's vision have fallen into disputes with one another over *how* he or she had been inspired. Jesus' life took the shape it did because he believed that God's Spirit was upon him and that he spoke for God. One sign of his prophetic identity is that controversy surrounded him during his life and continues to this day.

Among the prophets of the Abrahamic tradition, Muhammad targeted the issue of the Spirit and its impact on humanity more insistently than any other teacher. The Qur'an refashions the biblical source in Genesis 2, discussed in the last chapter, that describes how God created primal humanity. The Qur'an speaks of Allah breathing his own *Spirit* into him, rather than Soul, *and requiring that the angels fall down before the first human being as the container of Spirit* (Qur'an, Al Hijr 15.28-29):

> Look, your Lord said to the angels, I am about to create man from sounding clay, from mud molded into shape. When I have fashioned him and breathed into him my Spirit, fall down in recognition of him.

In Muhammad's revelation, man has access to divine Spirit in a way even the angels do not, and they are commanded to acknowledge that fact.

An angel named Iblis, however, cannot accept that a creature molded from clay could be his equal, much less his superior in possessing the Spirit. Iblis in the Qur'an is an alternative name for

Satan, a name that also appears. Iblis's primary rebellion, for which he is to be punished at the end of time, is this refusal to recognize the Spirit in man. This key contention is repeated in the Qur'an (Sad 38.71-85), together with the explanation that Iblis has no power whatever before the end of time except over those people who have lost their way to Allah.

The Spirit within man, directly breathed into him in the uniquely Qur'anic version of how humanity was created, becomes the fundamental explanation of faith in Islam. Spirit is the basis on which people can believe in Allah, while the denial of Spirit constitutes the primordial sin of Satan, and Satan's defining purpose is to spread that denial. But these efforts are vain when sincere believers are concerned, because Allah strengthens those who guard faith within their hearts with his Spirit (Al Mujadilah, 58.22). Spirit forms a perfect circle, from God to the believer and from the believer back to God, who gives ever more Spirit.

By contrast, Satan stands for the rejection of divine Spirit within human beings, and for breaking the connection between God and humanity. The clarity of that contrast comes through crisply in the Qur'an, which articulates a principle that underlies the conception of God's Spirit that the Abrahamic religions as a whole share. Just as the human Soul is the source of integrity and courage, Spirit gives that Soul direction and purpose. The rootedness of human action in God's continual creation of the world makes ethics, the science of right action, a matter of coordinating conduct with divine activity and divine intention as revealed by Spirit.

That fundamental link between ethics and Spirit explains why Satan, understood as a force that corrodes people's sense of the presence of God, becomes a pivotal figure in the Abrahamic traditions as a whole. The issue is not that Satan is arrayed against God

Images of violence, and even of warfare, punctuate Jesus' teaching, and justify referring to his commitment to what is traditionally called spiritual warfare. Jesus compared the life of a disciple to that of a king going to war with another king (Luke 14:31-32), an extension of his tough comparison of exorcism to plundering the house of a strong man.

These statements were not simply metaphors for Jesus. They were also part of his experience as a visionary prophet. When his disciples reported back to him regarding their own success in exorcism, he explained that they had "authority to trample over snakes and scorpions" (Luke 10:19), and spelled out the supernatural reason for this invulnerability of theirs. While the apostles were active, he said, "I observed Satan fall as lightning from the heaven" (Luke 10:18).

Yet Jesus' encounter with Satan was not simply a matter of easy victory. His experience of temptation at the hands the devil is proof of that. Jesus' popularity made him wonder whether he should take up the messianic challenge of his zealous supporters and attempt to wrest control of Israel from Rome. He wrestled with this question alone for days in the story called the Temptation (from the word *peirasmos* in Greek, which might be rendered as "test"). From the top of Mount Hermon, Jesus could see—as anyone might see today in good weather—the Sea of Galilee and the Jordan Valley to the south, and Galilee and the Mediterranean coast to the west. These were all the kingdoms of this world that mattered to Jesus. He later told his disciples that he had very nearly given in to the idea of a direct, military assault on Herod Antipas, the governor who had been Jesus' nemesis in Galilee.

Knowing the power of God meant knowing the temptations of Satan: to rule people through their hunger for bread, their awe over signs and wonders, their fear of power (Matthew 4:1-11; Luke 4:1-13). As for the Rabbis who spoke from experience about meditating on God and his infinite power, so for Jesus—there was exhilaration and danger in knowing the divine presence. The Transfiguration on Mount Hermon had shown Jesus and his disciples that he was God's Son: who then could deny such a teacher the power to rule?

The visions involved in the narrative of Jesus' Temptation suggest an advanced stage of Jesus' mystical practice. As a faithful Son of God, Jesus insisted against Satan that his miracles and signs were a reflection of God's power, not his own. Satan's pressure on Jesus to dominate others was in Aramaic a *nisyona*, a "temptation," a "test" or an occasion of being pressed to the point of being disloyal. The earliest form of "The Lord's Prayer," Jesus' characteristic approach to God, was completed in the dark night of Satan's temptation:

> My father,
>> your name will be sanctified, your Kingdom will come:
> Give me today the bread that is coming,
>> and release me my debts—not bring me to the test!

Temptation was constant in Jesus' life, and he conveyed to his disciples the necessity of resisting it, not simply with one's own strength, but in prayer. Jesus had broken barriers of convention and prejudice, and he needed to create his own personal form of prayer as a means of distinguishing the transcendent from the temporal, productive transgressions from personal exaltation.

The disciples too would be tempted to confuse God's Kingdom with their own power, especially as Jesus conveyed his personal visions to them and initiated them into his belief in how God was transforming the world. The heightened sense of the necessity of resistance to false impulses, common to the teaching of Jesus and Muhammad, derived from their acute insight that, without spiritual warfare, the disclosure of God's presence within a prophet could become a license of his or her own agenda.

Yet the language of warfare should not be permitted to give the impression that the Spirit in Jesus' view, or Muhammad's, was merely a matter of opposition. The whole point of resisting Satan is that Satan excludes or denies the deep connection between humanity and Spirit, which prophecy in every age has been designed to reawaken.

Paul was even more skillful than Jesus in explaining how this connection was designed to work. Writing during the year 56 C.E. to churches in Corinth, Paul explained that the Spirit is how God discloses himself, and at the same time amounts to a force that searches God out *on behalf* of humanity (1 Corinthians 2:10-11):

> But to us God has uncovered by his Spirit, because the Spirit searches all things, even the depths of God. Because who among men knows the thoughts of a man except the spirit of the man which is in him? So also no one has known the thoughts of God except the Spirit of God.

Paul goes on to speak of his profound sense of the link between divine and human sensibility, expressing himself in the idiom of Proverbs, but using the term "mind," rather than "Wisdom:" (1 Corinthians 2:14-16):

> A man of soul does not receive what comes of the Spirit of God, because it is foolishness to him, and he is not able to know, because they are judged spiritually. But the spiritual man judges all, and is himself judged by no one. For who has known the

Lord's mind; who will instruct him? But we have the mind of
Christ.

Here Paul shows how radical his view was that Spirit connects
God and humanity, and powerfully explains a difference that is all
too frequently glossed over: the difference between Soul and Spirit.

Spirit within a human being is not merely a matter of personal
identity, of Soul, but conveys the eternal reality of God. For that
reason, Paul conceives of people who are resurrected from the
dead as being a "spiritual body:" their whole substance is divine,
like God's own Spirit. Once a matter of flesh and Soul, human
identity is to be transformed into pure Spirit (1 Corinthians 15:42-
44).

For Paul as for great prophets of Spirit after him, the courage of
the Soul, a matter of basic human integrity, was ultimately completed by Spirit, the force of God that gives human action its creative and ethical impetus. Whatever resisted that destiny seemed
to Paul, as to the biblical tradition generally, to belong to the world
of the demonic—quasi-spiritual impulses that keep people from
what they had always been meant to be by God.

Spirit's power in Paul's mind and practice was worked out by
means of exorcism: the inrushing force of the divine Kingdom
destroyed the demons' fortresses on the earth. This miraculous
power played out, Paul said, in his struggle with Satan. Satan
could disguise himself as an angel of light according to Paul, as he
says in a statement reminiscent of Jesus' Temptation (2 Corinthians
11:14). Paul's campaign was part of the underlying, spiritual warfare that was more fateful than any war the world could wage
(2 Corinthians 10:4): "For the weapons of our warfare are not of
flesh, but powerful in God for the demolition of strongholds." The

struggle for humanity was an intellectual and emotional combat that centered on the conquest of evil in the human heart.

Paul's claim of authority over Satan goes back to Jesus' vision: Jesus saw Satan fall (Luke 10:18) when his apostles commanded unclean spirits to depart. However confident these assertions, Jesus also finds himself tested by Satan (Matthew 4:1-11; Mark 1:12-13; Luke 4:1-13), and Paul openly admits (2 Corinthians 12:7-9) that he could never free himself of the "thorn in the flesh, an angel of Satan."

Neither Paul nor Jesus ever claimed an effortless victory over evil. They saw the struggle with evil, whether in the physical world or within one's Soul, as a sign of the Kingdom's arrival. For Paul, as for Jesus, divine Spirit, not personal power, overcame evil and the rude force of the exorcist empowered by the Spirit meant more than elaborate techniques of magic. So Jesus is depicted as entering into shouting matches with the unclean spirits (Mark 5:1-17), and Paul speaks of battling at the strongholds of Satan (2 Corinthians 10:4).

The drive of Spirit, its sense of purpose in unifying a person with God, and people with one another as they are united with God, represents the purpose that gives the courage of Soul a direction. Yet both courage and purpose, of course, need something more to become real. Action and strategy alone will bring them into the world of human affairs, the stage where courage is proven, or not, and purpose emerges as a unifying blessing, or the reverse, depending on its impact on the people around us. For that reason, the spirituality of transformation, as practiced by Jesus as well as his predecessors and his successors, was rooted in the strategy of planting God's Kingdom in this world.

Struggling for how to work with the direction and force of the Spirit is obviously a deep challenge. It demands being in touch with the true nature of one's Soul but then goes beyond the limits we set on our own actions on the basis of who we understand ourselves to be. Just as we can usually be ourselves best in community, as we discussed in the last chapter, so community is often the place where, having been accepted as we are, we can also press for changes in ourselves and one another on the basis of a shared discernment of Spirit.

The discernment of Spirit, complete with spiritual warfare and a sense of finding oneself empowered and transformed, is a powerful force, and yet it does not only occur as a matter of our intention. "The Spirit blows where it wants," Jesus said, playing on "wind" as another possible meaning of *ruach*, "and you hear only the sound of it, but you do not know whence it comes or where it goes" (John 3:8). In the midst of the most ordinary routines, moments of spiritual breakthrough can and do occur unpredictably.

Years ago the leaders of my faith community, the trustees of the church, found themselves in disagreement over their investments. Disputes of this kind are common and quickly create the feeling that they will be interminable. A member of the congregation had left us his house in his will, since he had no heirs. So the trustees became responsible for a small endowment, a responsibility they had never had before. At first, they simply put the funds in a bank; but then they realized that market investments would be more productive, and one of the trustees, a skilled investor, began to acquire common stock.

The success of some of the stocks became the source of dispute. Should a church profit from the dividends and the increased value of tobacco stocks? The balance is often difficult to strike between wishing to do well for an organization with investments and the ethical aims of the organization itself. Probably no single answer or philosophy of investing can create the right balance for all organizations all the time. The disagreement among our trustees was vigorous, and sometimes divisive.

But then something happened that, in an unexpected way from an unexpected quarter, solved the problem. One of the trustees was (and is) a highly successful lawyer, with an impressive legal *and* practical mind. He was not convinced by the ethical arguments of those who wished to divest from stocks that involved tobacco, and the irony was not lost on him that at least one of those who wished to divest continued to smoke cigarettes.

Irony can go in many directions, and in Wayne's case it became surprisingly productive, instead of merely sarcastic. One Sunday, speaking not only to the trustees but also within a group enjoying coffee and fellowship after the morning service, he blurted out, "How can you argue against investing in a product people are addicted to? It is the perfect investment!" At one level, he said this quite seriously, and he answered a few objections to his remark. But as he engaged in conversation, the smile on his face became broader and broader.

Instead of making an earnest argument about investing or not investing, he had hit on the humor of the situation, as showing how wide the gap had grown between where we placed our financial bets and how we would like to see people live their lives. This productive irony made connections quickly and intuitively, without the clouds of bad feeling that can accompany arguments about issues of this kind.

Sometimes I was simultaneously shocked and delighted by how dark Wayne's humor could become. On another Sunday, we were discussing the plan for reforming the American health system that the Clinton Administration was in the process of developing. Wayne pointed out that the country could save a great deal of money on both Medicare and Social Security by reverting to the practice of the American military during the Second World War: just hand out free cigarettes with retirement payments. Not everyone found this funny, but my sense of humor remains bent enough to enjoy Wayne's joke to this day.

Wayne's humor, whether or not you could always approve of its taste, made a consistent connection between assessments of financial benefit and the good of human beings. Without making any formal argument about our investments, he did more than any single person to move the church's endowment out of tobacco stock.

Once we had made changes in the stocks we owned, a series of legal rulings pushed the value of tobacco stocks down. Another irony had emerged: as it turned out, what we had done on ethical grounds had proved to be financially prudent. Wayne, however, never turned that new irony into a joke. He stood by his wisecracks about tobacco products.

The voice of ancient Israelite prophecy also included humor, some of it biting. During the nine century B.C.E. Elijah mocked the prophets of Baal, asking why their prayers had not been answered. Perhaps, he suggested, Baal had departed on a little holiday or was taking a nap (1 Kings 18:27). That kind of ridicule became a theme among the prophets of Israel. The Spirit makes connections between what people say and what they do, between the kind of worship they engage in and the God they think to serve, between what they do with their money or other tangible resources and the good they claim to do in the world. The Spirit forges those links in the social world, just as God's Spirit forms the connective tissue of the universe we live in. For that reason, the agents of Spirit, the prophets in age after age, often have to call attention to the absurd inconsistencies human communities fall into when they lose touch with the connection between who they truly are and what they do. Gentle as a dove in her infusion of purpose, the Spirit also empowers her people to become warriors in the service of their holy calling.

3
Kingdom

In all Jesus' teaching, no single concept is more important, more central, or more resonant than the Kingdom of God. The Kingdom of God also figures as a vital concept within the Scriptures of Israel. By referring to the Kingdom, Jesus and prophets before him focused on God as the king of the universe, the fundamental energy behind all that is, and on God's role in shaping human experience to its best ends. While Spirit is the creative power and design of God, the Kingdom is God's force within human affairs in particular. As an emissary of Spirit, Jesus embraced the prophetic principle of the Kingdom and gave the concept his own unique meaning.

The promise of God's Kingdom is that people will finally come to realize divine justice and peace in all that they do, putting into action *with one another* the righteousness they see in God. The Kingdom is a matter of both perceiving God's will and doing God's will—on earth as it is in heaven.

In the ancient world, any kind of effective government had its king; referring to "the Kingdom of God" in no sense preferred monarchy to democracy. After all, modern ideas of democracy took millennia to work out.[1] To speak of a Kingdom where God was in charge implied that he removed all the consequences of human greed and tyranny, and replaced them with a common passion for divine justice. So the Kingdom is definitely a matter of vision, of perceiving God's justice in the present and anticipating its complete emergence in the future, but it is also a matter of ethics, of what we do to make God's will work. Jesus made the Kingdom of God the center of his preaching as well as of his activity, and it remains the pivot of Christian theology.

Because the Kingdom is a *power* exerted *within* human beings, and not an entity alien to them, to understand it requires both more and less than a simple definition. That is why people often find the Kingdom of God difficult to grasp: it is not just an idea that needs to be defined, and not just a standard of ethics that needs to be enacted, but combines the two, vision and practice.

As in the case of any force for justice, we need to be prepared to see and feel the Kingdom as it influences people if they wish to be part of it. Racial equality in the United States, for example, has not just been a matter of passing legislation or making philosophical arguments. Both of those activities have naturally been involved, but personal attitudes, intimate emotions, and a willingness to change the habits of local communities have also proved crucial. Similarly, reducing the Kingdom to a static concept such as "God's plan for humanity," or "the reward of the just," oversimplifies what is involved and makes the Kingdom seem too abstract. The Kingdom includes plans and rewards but cannot be limited to them, because it refers to the *whole process* by which God shapes humanity. That is why it takes *more* than a definition to understand the Kingdom of God.

As a process, however, the Kingdom is also *less* a matter of intellectual definition than it is an activity, both God's and humanity's. Whether in present experience or in hope for the future, ancient

Israelites saw the Kingdom of God as active within their lives. In five distinct ways, all closely related to one another, they perceived that God made himself available to people in activities they could join themselves to. The book of Psalms clearly reflects these ways of seeing the Kingdom as a process, and Jesus also taught that the Kingdom could be known in these five ways.

Both the Psalms and Jesus referred to the Kingdom according to how its force could be perceived, and how that force would shape all of human life with the active cooperation of God's people. The five ways in which the Kingdom can be known are (1) in time, as a hope for the future, (2) in space, as a change from conflict to harmony, (3) in human behavior, as the desire for justice, (4) in the human heart, as pure dedication to God, and (5) in human imagination, as it reaches out to include others in its vision of peace. All of these ways are included in the Kingdom, and none of them can be ignored without distorting the significance of this basic prophetic conception.

First, because God's creativity reaches into a future that is beyond human control, the Kingdom of God is also beyond the immediate comprehension of any living thing. A time of universal justice could only be eschatological, that is, belonging to the very last phase (the *eskhaton* in Greek) of human development. Yet the justice that is to be completed in the Kingdom is at least partially known in the present. We all know what justice is, even if we know that people fall short of its standards, and even when we might not be able to specify what is right beyond an inchoate sense of what is fair.

The book of Psalms portrays the Kingdom as so near as to seem present in time and tangible, and yet ultimate and distant from the point of view of what its full disclosure will be like (Psalm 96:10):

Say among the nations that the LORD reigns.
   The world is established, so as not to move:
   he shall judge the peoples with equity.

When God judges, all peoples will finally know the truth that is even now realized and celebrated by those who worship God. Those who sing, the group that joins together in order to recite this psalm, recognize now—not just in the future—that "the world is established, so as not to move" by God. The wonderful order of the universe invites the Psalmic community to rejoice in God's power in the present, and to anticipate his full revelation in the future. Biblical eschatology lives in the tension between what can be perceived now as a partial reality and the realization that is not yet disclosed in its fullness.

Second, just as the Kingdom cannot be contained by time, but stretches eschatologically to include both the present and the future, so it is transcendent in space. The usual setting of Israel's praise is in the Temple, where the psalms were typically sung. But every part of the creation will come to acknowledge what is known in the Temple (Psalm 145:10-13):

All your creatures will give you thanks, LORD,
   and your faithful will bless you;
they shall speak of the glory of your Kingdom,
   and tell of your might,
to make your mighty deeds known to the sons of men,
   and the glorious splendor of his Kingdom.
Your Kingdom is an everlasting Kingdom,
   and your rule in every generation.

All his creatures are to give thanks to the LORD, but it is his faithful in particular who are said to bless him.

What is rehearsed in the Temple, the "strength of the fearful acts" of God, is to be acknowledged by humanity as a whole (Psalm 145:6), without their inveterate conflicts. The ancient prophetic image of the peaceable Kingdom—where wolf and lamb, leopard and goat, calf and lion will dwell together (Isaiah 11:6)— derives from this same underlying vision of what will be possible when (Isaiah 11:9) "the earth shall be filled with the knowledge of God as the waters cover the seas." The transcendence of the Kingdom means the resolution of disputes and the dissolution of violence.

Third, the Kingdom is an insistent ethical force that will ultimately prevail. God's Kingdom is always righteous but attains to a consummation when righteousness is the rule of the day (see Psalm 10:15-16):

> Break the arm of the wicked, and evil;
>> search out his wickedness until it cannot be found!
> The LORD is king forever and ever;
>> the nations perish from his earth!

The punishment of the wicked is the dark side of the blessing of the poor. In order to be realized, the vindication of the meek, the fatherless, and the oppressed (in vv. 17, 18a of this psalm) requires a reversal in the fortunes of those who do evil and oppress the innocent. Judgment features centrally in expectations of the Kingdom of God. Justice means the removal of tyranny as well as the triumph of innocence. The wolf who learns to dwell with the lamb is obviously a new kind of wolf, and the Kingdom brings with it the righteousness to effect its change.

Fourth, human entry into the Kingdom depends upon what people are at their core, as well as the righteousness they enact. Psalm

24 poses, and then answers, a question that is central to the religion of Israel as reflected in the biblical tradition (Psalm 24:3-4):

> Who will ascend the mount of the LORD,
>   and who will stand in his holy place?
> The innocent of hands and pure of heart,
>   who has not lifted up his Soul to vanity,
>   and has not sworn deceitfully.

The point is that purity is affected by one's attitudes and motivations as well as by the practices of purification (such as bathing) that were conventionally a part of ascending the mount of the Temple. Just as hope in God's future and commitment to his power to transform human life with justice are dimensions by which the Kingdom of God makes itself known, so there is also a dimension of purity. Devotion to the presence of God, by using the best means available to make us personally involved with God's will and purpose, features prominently as a way of experiencing the Kingdom and putting it into action.

Fifth, the book of Psalms evokes how the recognition of the Kingdom is to radiate outward from its center, the presence of God in the Temple. Instead of portraying Israel as being at odds with the nations (the Gentiles), one psalm identifies "the people of the God of Abraham" as being "the nobles of the peoples" (Psalm 47:9). In this prophetic hymn, humanity at large gathers to acknowledge the power of God, with Israel at the center of a larger whole:

> The nobles of the peoples are gathered,
>   the people of the God of Abraham;
> for the shields of the earth are God's.
>   He is highly exalted!

Israel is the nucleus of the larger group of those who recognize the God of Jacob. From its center, the power of the Kingdom is to stream outward to include peoples beyond the commonly acknowledged range of Israel within the recognition of God's power.

Jesus articulated all five of these ways of seeing and sensing the Kingdom, because he understood that they conveyed the mystery of how God shapes the human world and brings it to consummation. He taught his disciples to pray to God in regard to the eschatological future, "Your Kingdom will come" (Matthew 6:10; Luke 11:2). He hoped for the Kingdom to be fully present among all people. In Aramaic, he really said that the Kingdom "will" come, not merely that he wished for it to come (as in the conventional but rather weak rendering "Thy Kingdom come").[2] In the same way that God's presence can be sensed now, he taught, his followers should also welcome its coming in the future as an eschatological *fact*.

Jesus' belief that the Kingdom is transcendent, capable of displacing other powers, comes through clearly in one of his most famous sayings (Matthew 12:28; Luke 11:20), "If I by the Spirit of God cast out demons, then the Kingdom of God has arrived upon you." Exorcism for Jesus was not an esoteric or magical practice but a matter of confronting evil with the power of divine justice and bringing about immediate transformation. In Jesus' teaching, this transformation was usually realized in terms of purity (as we will describe further in a moment, under the fourth dimension of the Kingdom's activity). Spirit, the creative power of God, joined with the Kingdom, God's purpose for humanity, to take people out of the control of the interior, divisive impulses that might easily ruin their lives, and restore them to become the autonomous human beings that God had created.

Entry into the Kingdom is the dominant image in Jesus' famous statement about wealth (Matthew 19:23-24; Mark 10:23-25; Luke 18:24-25), as well as in other demands for justice: "Easier for a camel to wriggle through the eye of a needle than for a rich man to enter the Kingdom of God." In this and in other teachings, Jesus insisted that God's justice reversed many of the conventional standards of this world.

Jesus' well-known parable of a feast to which the host makes surprising, insistent invitations—and equally categorical exclusions—also voices a radical view of righteousness (see Matthew 22:1-14; Luke 14:16-24). God is portrayed as celebrating in his Kingdom with those who would join him, and as refusing to include those who have rejected the ethical means of entering his kingdom. Because Jesus was and is rightly known as the supreme teacher of divine love, the judgmental aspect of his teaching, which speaks of punishing resistance to the Kingdom, is frequently—and all too conveniently—ignored. Indeed, the term "judgmental" has come to be used in modern English as a pejorative, as if judgment itself were somehow beneath the nature of God. But there is finally no compromise in God's love: it supersedes what would resist it and for that reason exercises loving judgment.

This dedication to justice, the third dimension of the Kingdom, leads on naturally to the fourth: Jesus needed to cope in his daily contacts with the issue of defilement as one member of Israel (with a certain set of practices) met with another member of Israel (with another set of practices). To deal with that question, a single aphorism of Jesus was precisely designed: "There is nothing outside the man proceeding into him that defiles him, but what proceeds out of the man is what defiles the man" (Mark 7:15). This principle sees people as inherently pure, so that every Israelite should be willing to accept every other Israelite. That resolved a practical issue for Jesus' highly mobile followers, and at a later stage opened the possibility of the inclusion of non-Jews within his movement. But the principle also raises the question of how people can become impure.

Jesus typically called demons "unclean spirits." For Jesus, people taken on their own were as clean as God had made Adam and Eve. If a person became unclean or impure, that was not because of contact with exterior objects. Instead, impurity was a disturbance within that person's own Spirit, the "unclean spirit" that made him or her want to be impure, and even inflict self-harm. The description of the man with a legion of demons (see Mark 5:1-20) precisely captures the sense of a person turned against himself as a result of a compulsion that took over the control that rightly should have been exercised by his own mind.

In Jesus' perspective, uncleanness arrived not from material contagion at all, but from the disturbed desire people conceive to pollute and do harm to themselves. Uncleanness had to be dealt with in the inward, spiritual personality of those afflicted. Jesus believed that God's Spirit was a far more vital force than the unclean spirits that disturbed humanity. Against demonic infection a greater counter-contagion could prevail, the positive energy of God's purity.[3]

Fifth and finally, in the course of Jesus' occupation of the Temple, Jesus articulated the dimension of the Kingdom's radiance (Mark 11:17), "My house shall be called a house of prayer for all the nations, but you have made it a den of thieves." Jesus objected to the presence of merchants who had been given permission to sell sacrificial animals in the vast outer court of the Temple. His objection was based on his own view of purity, grounded in a commitment to realize prophetic predictions such as Zechariah 14:16-21: Israel should offer, not priest's produce for which they bartered, but their own sacrifices that they brought into the Temple, and ultimately all the peoples of the earth should be able to worship in Jerusalem. He and his followers drove the animals and the sellers out of the great court with the use of force.

In Jesus' teaching, the five coordinates of the Kingdom become the dynamics of the Kingdom: the ways in which God is active with his people emerge as principles of human action, including violent action in the case of what Jesus did in the Temple. Because God as Kingdom is active, response to him is active, not only cognitive. The Kingdom of God is a matter of performing the hopeful dynamics of God's revelation to his people. For that reason, Jesus' teaching was not only a matter of making statements, however carefully crafted and remembered. He also engaged in characteristic activities, a conscious performance of the Kingdom, which invited Israel to enter into the reality that he also portrayed in words. Once experience *and* activity are understood to be the terms of reference of the Kingdom, what one actually does is also an instrument of its revelation, an aspect of its radiance. Jesus' awareness of that caused him to act as programmatically as he spoke, to make his total activity into a parable of the Kingdom.

One of the most profound challenges of Jesus' teaching as a whole is that the Kingdom of God is not merely for him to perform but for all who perceive it. Jesus honed a type of speech well known within the Judaism of his time, the parable, to convey both the perception of the Kingdom and the imperative to act upon one's perception.

The Hebrew term rendered by Greek *parabole* and English "parable" is *mashal*, which basically refers to a "comparison." For that reason, the genre as a whole explores metaphorical possibilities. The book of Proverbs, for example, is called *meshalim* in Hebrew, "comparisons"—illustrating that the term *mashal* has a wider sense than any single term in English conveys.

The book of Ezekiel develops this wide range of Hebrew meaning. In the name of the LORD, the prophet says, "There is nothing for you in parabling [*moshlim*] this parable [*mashal*], The fathers ate sour grapes and the children's teeth stand on edge" (Ezekiel 18:2). Obviously, there is no requirement of a strong narrative element within the metaphorical image for the "parable" to be considered as such. Its meaning is transparent as soon as the metaphor is understood. Ezekiel uses this proverbial metaphor of sour grapes to object to the idea that God punishes children for their parents' sins.

Yet within the same book of Ezekiel, parables can be developed in an elaborate way, so that they may be called allegories (which come complete with explanations): the fate of Israel between Babylon and Egypt, for example, is addressed by comparison to two eagles and a sprig of cedar (Ezekiel 17). It is fortunate the chapter includes interpretation, because this particular parable (which is translated "allegory" at 17:2 in the New Revised Standard Version) is complicated, opaque, and unrealistic. Nathan's parable of the ewe lamb in 2 Samuel 12:1-15 is a more successful development of narrative allegory and interpretation; it is not in the least surprising that David got the point of the parable and understood that his adultery with Bathsheba, the wife of Uriah, would not go unpunished.

Jesus was known as a master of the genre of parable in its full extent, from simple adage to complicated—sometimes, as we shall see, even surreal—narrative. Of course, the parabolic sayings attributed to Jesus underwent considerable embellishment during the course of transmission before and as they were written down in the Gospels. But the primary interest here is not in parsing the difference between what Jesus said and commentary on what he said, but in the depth and range of his parables as declarations of the Kingdom.

Answering the charge that his exorcisms were performed by the power of Satan, Jesus replied with his observation, discussed in the last chapter, that no kingdom or house divided against itself can stand (Mark 3:22-25; Matthew 12:24-25; Luke 11:15-17). That vivid maxim has lived on within the proverbial tradition of many languages. But the meaning intended by Jesus is sometimes reversed. When in 1858 Abraham Lincoln gave his speech about a house divided against itself, for example, his point was that the United States could not endure half slave and half free.[4] Lincoln obviously wanted the Union to endure—but Jesus couldn't wait for Satan's house to fall. Jesus' point was that his exorcisms, empowered by God's Spirit, replaced Satan's authority with God's Kingdom. Obviously, he said, Satan would not conspire in his own downfall.

The Gospels underline Jesus' expectation of spiritual régime change by including a parable with a narrative element, the comparison with attempting to rob a strong man's house (Mark 3:27; Matthew 12:29, developed more fully in Luke 11:21-22). Here, too, part of the force of the comparison lies in its surprising sympathy—with the thief, rather than with the householder. Jesus compares himself to a skillful burglar and Satan to a man so wealthy he deserves the theft that is coming his way.

The parables of the divided house and of the thief with a good strategy share a pointed anticipation of Satan's defeat, as a consequence of the Kingdom's victory. They also show how easily a parable that is basically a simple metaphor might develop into a parable with a strong narrative element. For that reason, unlike some recent treatments, no hard and fast distinction is suggested here between metaphorical and narrative parables, since a single *mashal* can easily participate in several features of the genre overall.

The parable of the sower develops the narrative element that was perennially an option within the genre of parable, complete with an interpretation of the allegory (Mark 4:3-8, 13-20; Matthew 13:3-8, 18-23; Luke 8:5-8, 11-15). No less instructive than the parable in Ezekiel 17, the consistent usage of a metaphor is as striking here as in other parables of Jesus.

In his remarkable book on rabbinic parables in relation to Jesus', David Flusser has debunked the widely held generalization that Rabbinic parables were always exegetical, in the nature of commentaries.[5] He cites as an example the parable of Yochanan ben Zakkai (in the Babylonian Talmud, Shabbath 153a). Yochanan told of a king who invited his servants to a feast, without announcing the hour of the meal. Wise servants attired themselves properly, and waited at the door of the king's house. Foolish servants expected definite signs that the meal was being readied, and went about their work until they should see preparations under way. Then the king appeared without further notice. While the wise servants enjoyed a fine meal, the foolish, work-soiled servants were made to stand and watch.

The motif of a festal banquet is also central within Jesus' parables and sayings, and the Matthean parable of the wedding feast

(Matthew 22:1-14, cf. Luke 14:16-24) especially invites comparison with Yochanan's. Matthew's subplot concerning the appropriate wedding garment (vv. 11-13) provides another point of similarity. Still, the meanings generated by the two parables are distinctive. Where Yochanan speaks of servants who either are or are not prudent in their assessment of the king's capacity, Jesus speaks of guests invited to a feast who respond with extraordinarily bad and finally violent behavior that is answered in kind. Beneath that distinction, of course, there is a thematic similarity. Readiness to accept and act upon the invitation is imperative, since the king is none other than God.

Each parable urges a particular kind of response upon the hearer. Yochanan's narrative involves dropping normal obligations to await God's promised banquet, while Jesus' parable of recalcitrant guests is more fraught in its warning against obstinacy. Perhaps most importantly, comparison with Rabbinic parables reveals what has frequently been overlooked in Jesus' parables: surrealism is possible within the genre, from Ezekiel through Jesus and on to Yochanan ben Zakkai. Parables are not just lively stories taken from nature; the point can often turn on what is striking, peculiar, or unpredictable.

Even in Jesus' parables of growth, elements of hyperbole are plain. In the narrative of the man, the seed, and the earth (Mark 4:26-29), action is abrupt and unmotivated. The man sleeps for no stated reason, and puts in his sickle "immediately;" the seed sprouts in no time, and the earth produces "as of itself." Similarly, mustard seed becomes a "tree" (Matthew 13:31-32; Luke 13:18-19), or makes "big branches" (Mark 4:30-32) without an interval of time being indicated. The point lies in the contrast of beginning and result, miraculous transformation rather than predictable process.

The hyperbolic comparison of start and finish is also evident in the parable of the leaven (Matthew 13:33; Luke 13:20-21). The parables of the hidden treasure and the pearl (Matthew 13:44-46) are surprising, rather than hyperbolic, when they concern the discovery of what is valuable, but the reaction of those who find them, in selling everything to acquire them, is exaggerated. In these cases, also, ethical themes are especially conveyed by the *least realistic* motifs.

Like the prophets, Jesus taught his hearers how to see the Kingdom, as well as how to act on the basis of what they saw. Vision—the capacity to perceive God actively at work—is the prophetic foundation of calling people to work with God. Just as Lao-Tsu is Jesus' greatest predecessor in regard to the Soul, and Muhammad took prophetic teaching in regard to Spirit to a new level of articulation, so Moses stands out as the most comprehensive teacher of God's Kingdom in terms of putting vision into action.

In the Judaism of Jesus' time, it was said that every Israelite, every day, took "the yoke of the Kingdom of heaven" upon him or herself (see the Mishnah, Berakhoth 2:2). The underlying image puts Israelites in the role of beasts of burden, yoked in harness in order to discharge the duties for which they were intended. Then, if they do in fact accept obedience, they prove themselves innocent of the accusation leveled at them by Isaiah, "The ox knows his owner, and the ass his master's trough; Israel does not know, my people do not consider" (Isaiah 1:3).

The moment of harnessing oneself to God's Kingdom was at the time of reciting one of the principal texts of Judaism, the *Shema' Yisrael* (from its first words, those of Deuteronomy 6:4-7, "Hear, Israel"):

Hear, Israel, the LORD our God, the LORD is one, and you shall love the LORD your God with all your heart and with all your soul and with all your strength. And these words that I command you today shall be upon your heart, and you shall repeat them to your sons and speak of them when you sit in your house and when you walk on the way, and when you lie down and when you rise up.

When asked about the "first commandment" in the Torah, of course, this is the one Jesus cited (Mark 12:29-30). In addition, Jesus urged his followers to learn from him by means of a famous saying, "because my yoke is good and my burden is light" (Matthew 11:30). The motif of the good or "easy" yoke (another way of translating the Greek term *khrestos*) is a shared metaphor that links Jesus with the Rabbinic language that emerged in documents from the second century and later, although their oral roots sometimes reach into the time prior to Jesus.

Yet in this case as in others, the sharing of language, when viewed contextually, reveals vital differences. The Rabbinic "yoke" connects the Israelite to the Torah; Jesus' "yoke" links the disciple to God's Kingdom. Profound lines of cleavage, and of controversy, emanate from that distinction. Before we investigate them, however, we should see how Jesus' emphasis on the Kingdom of God grew out of Israelite religion, and *then* how this emphasis departed from the focus on the Torah that the Rabbis made their norm.

At one point in the Hebrew Bible, Moses is described as seeing God. In fact, Moses is the leader of a large group of Israelites at the moment of the vision. Exodus 24 describes this unusual event. Moses builds an altar of twelve stone pillars at the foot of the mount Sinai. He pours blood on the altar, and then reads from the Book of the Covenant, the sacred contract between God and his people revealed to him on Sinai. When the people promise to obey the Covenant, Moses also pours blood over the people, saying "Look, the blood of the Covenant that the LORD has cut with you by all these words" (Exodus 24:4-8). Then the visionary text follows (Exodus 24:9-10):

> Moses went up with Aaron, Nadab, and Abihu and seventy of the elders of Israel, and they saw the God of Israel, and under his feet like a work of sapphire pavement and like the essence of heaven in clarity. Upon the nobles of the sons of Israel he did not send his hand; they saw God, and ate and drank.

The economy of this text does not in any way prevent it from detailing a profound vision, a contact with the divine on the part of the best representatives of the people.

The book of Exodus later has God tell Moses, "You cannot see my face" but that proves not to be an absolute prohibition of seeing God, even in this later chapter, because Moses does perceive the divine form (Exodus 33:19-23). Taken together, the two chapters in Exodus (chapters 24 and 33) suggest that the vision of God is partial, and not like ordinary sight, but that it is possible, although difficult and dangerous. What Moses and the elders perceived in Exodus 24 was not God personally, but the throne of God.

After the time of Moses the religion of Israel focused increasingly on the throne of God as his powerful, spiritual presence. Although that force could be perceived by human beings, contact with the divine was more like being known by God than knowing God oneself. God's throne was conceived of as being movable, a chariot rather than a fixed point in time and space, because God might disclose himself at any moment, in any place. At the time of the death of Elijah, according to 2 Kings (2:11), he and his student Elisha are walking, when, "Look, a chariot of fire and horses of fire, separated the two of them, and Elijah went up in a whirlwind into heaven." Moses and Elijah both became prime Israelite symbols of the vision of God, and both were said to have encounters with God on mountains (compare Exodus 24 and 1 Kings 19). When Jesus encountered God, and conveyed his experience to his disciples, the narrative delves into this rich symbolism.

The Transfiguration (Matthew 16:28–17:13; Mark 9:1-13; Luke 9:27-36) is one of the most majestic stories in the Gospels, both beautifully and simply written. Jesus is transformed before Peter, James, and John into a gleaming white figure, speaking with Moses and Elijah. Jesus' visions were not merely private; years of communal meditation made what he saw and experienced vivid to his own disciples, as well. On Mount Hermon, Jesus followed in the footsteps of Moses, who took three of his followers (Aaron, Nadab, and Abihu) up Mount Sinai, where they ate and drank to celebrate their vision of the God of Israel on his sapphire throne (see Exodus 24:1-11).

But unlike what happened with Moses' followers on Mount Sinai, Jesus' disciples, covered by a shining cloud of glory, hear a voice, "This is my Son, the beloved, in whom I take pleasure: hear him," and when the cloud passed they found Jesus without Moses and Elijah, standing alone as God's Son (Matthew 17:5). Divine "Son" was the same designation Jesus had heard during his immersion with John the Baptist; now his own disciples saw and heard the truth of his own vision.

As in the earlier case with John, the voice that came after the luminous cloud in the Transfiguration did not speak in the exclusive language of the later doctrine of the Trinity, which made Jesus into the only (and only possible) "Son of God." Rather, the point was that the same Spirit that had animated Moses and Elijah was present in Jesus, and that he could pass on that Spirit to his followers, each of whom could also become a "Son."

In the midst of seeing the vision and hearing the divine voice, Peter offered to build three "huts," or *sukkoth* (as they would be called in Hebrew), for Jesus and Moses and Elijah, and Mark's Gospel presents that as a witless suggestion (Mark 9:5-6):

> Peter responded and says to Jesus, Rabbi, it is fine for us to be here, and we shall build three huts: one for you and one for Moses and one for Elijah. For he did not know how he should respond, because they were terrified.

That typifies what frequently happened during the formation of the Gospels. When the significance of Judaic symbolism was forgotten, this was attributed to the ineptitude of the apostles, rather than the cultural amnesia of the Church.

In the present case, Peter's remark referred to the fact that a great feast known as Sukkoth or Tabernacles was coming. That feast, the agricultural harvest of the autumn, and therefore the largest of the year, celebrated the prosperity of the land and remembered the time when Israel lived in the wilderness in huts prior to their entry into Canaan.[6] Israelites actually set up huts and lived in them during the feast; the practice embodied the hope of living anew in communion with God.

Peter offered to set up huts so that Jesus, Moses, and Elijah would remain with the apostles and guide them to the fulfilled promise of the Kingdom. There is a touching quality about Peter's impulse to provide shelter for the visionary experience of God's presence. It is an exact indication that he, with James and John, had indeed joined Jesus in the vision of the divine throne or Chariot.

The Mishnah teaches that the Chariot should not be introduced to a person alone (Chagigah 2:1); the vision of the divine throne was fraught with danger. Some initiates died, some went mad, and still others fell prey to polytheism by meditating on the Throne incautiously (Chagigah 2:1-7 in Tosefta). It was part of his genius as a rabbi that Jesus led his disciples into a vision of the Chariot in a way that mobilized and safely transformed them. By sharing his vision with them, he shifted the center of his teaching away from what can be discerned of God's Kingdom on earth to what can be experienced of the heavenly reality of God's Throne.

The Transfiguration represents the mature development of Rabbi Jesus' visionary discipline; he was able not only to articulate his own vision but also to initiate others into its richness. In regard to the vision of God, in addition to the genre of parables, the book of Ezekiel—which includes a detailed description of God's Chariot in its opening chapter—exerted a powerful influence on Jesus. The reaction that had begun with the Spirit's address of him as "Son" exploded into the consciousness of his disciples. They now saw him as a living presence in the pantheon of Israel's prophets before God's Throne. Their rabbi stood within the creative fire that was creation's source, favored by the power of the thundering voice of God (see John 12:29). It must have seemed to them at that moment that all the hardships, struggles, and disappointments which following this man involved had finally found their reward in the intimacy with the divine presence that he gave them.

In Jesus' conception, this divine presence was the force behind the Kingdom of God. As he said to Peter, James, and John just before the Transfiguration, "There are some standing here who shall not taste death, until they see the Kingdom of God having come in power" (Mark 9:1, see Matthew 16:28; Luke 9:27). Both Moses and Elijah were thought in the Jewish tradition of this time to have been immortal; like Elijah taken up in God's chariot, Moses also was believed to have gone alive into heaven. In Jesus' conception, those who lived in God's presence, people such as Moses and Elijah (but also Abraham, Isaac, and Jacob, in Jesus' view), showed the way for humanity as a whole. "The Kingdom of God having come in power" expresses in a single phrase how Jesus anticipated that God would definitively transform the world and humanity in their present forms.

Genuine transformation is a frightening prospect. It involves altering the usual points of reference people use to know who they are, where they are, and what they can do to improve their lives. "The Kingdom of God having come in power" refers to a complete alteration of conventional reality. The phrase resonates with works that depict the apocalyptic dissolution of both social institutions and the tangible, physical world. The final chapter of the book of Zechariah, for example, predicted that Israel would envelop all the nations in an ultimate sacrifice on Mount Zion in the midst of warfare, destruction, earthquake, and plague. The Aramaic version of the book sets out that apocalypse in language like Jesus' (Targum Zechariah 14:9, with departures from the Hebrew text in italics):

> *And the Kingdom of the* LORD *shall be revealed* upon all *the inhabitants of* the earth; at that *time they shall serve before the* LORD *with one accord, for* his name *is established in the world; there is none apart from* him.

To Jesus, this expectation was not merely a matter of symbolism or an expectation that could be passively awaited. Instead, he actually acted upon the apocalyptic scenario of transformation, in order actively to join God in establishing his Kingdom.

Jesus' last public action—his intervention in the normal operation of the Temple in Jerusalem—enacted the prophecy of Zechariah, particularly in its Aramaic version (Targum Zechariah 14:21b): "and there shall never again be a *trader* in the *sanctuary* of the Lord of hosts at that *time*." Putting those words into practice also put Jesus into direct opposition to the high priest, Caiaphas, who had authorized the selling and buying inside the Temple that Jesus objected to violently. He intervened with force and threw out both the vendors and their animals (Matthew 21:12-17; Mark 11:11-18; Luke 19:45-48; John 2:13-20).

This act is the key to why Jesus was crucified by the Romans, who had put their prestige behind the *status quo* in the Temple. Although almost every claim ever asserted about Jesus has been subject to disputes (some sophisticated, some well intentioned but ill-advised, and some ideologically driven), the fact of his forceful intervention in the Temple is a matter of historical fact.[7]

More important than the details of Jesus' action for an understanding of the prophetic force he wished to unleash, however, is his total vision of the Kingdom, in which Zechariah's prophecy of the cleansing of the Temple of commerce played a part. Jesus assimilated Zechariah's vision into his own and made it a programmatic part of his action.

Three further key texts in Zechariah set out characteristic concerns of Jesus' message:

- Zechariah 8:7-8—Yahweh of armies says this: Look, I am saving my people from the east country and from the country of the setting sun, and I will bring them, and they shall dwell in the midst of Jerusalem, and they shall be to me for a people, and I shall be their God in truth and righteousness.

- Zechariah 8:16-17—These are the things you shall do: Speak truth, a man with his neighbor—truth! Judge a judgment of peace in your gates, and do not devise evil, a man against his neighbor, in your hearts, and don't love a lying oath—because all these I hate, Yahweh's speech.
- Zechariah 8:19—Yahweh of armies says this, The fast of the fourth month, and the fast of the fifth month, and the fast of the seventh month, and the fast of the tenth month shall be to the house of Judah for joy and festival and good times, and you shall love truth and peace.

Very often an antiquated misunderstanding arises in the minds of modern readers of the Bible. (Unfortunately, the error is even repeated by some writers who should know better.) A classic reductionist contrast portrays "the God of the Old Testament" as violent and vengeful, while Jesus preached "the God of mercy." But we have already seen that Jesus was willing to resort to violence, and these prophecies of Zechariah—themselves completely in line with other prophetic messages in the Hebrew Bible—show that Jesus was directly inspired by the Prophets.

When Jesus said that "Many shall come from east and west and recline in feasting with Abraham, Isaac, and Jacob in the Kingdom of God" (Matthew 8:11, cf. Luke 13:29), he echoed Zechariah (Zechariah 8:7-8). When he spoke of love of God and love of neighbor as summing up the Torah (Matthew 22:34-40; Mark 12:28-34; Luke 10:27-28), he developed a principle Zechariah had stated (Zechariah 8:16-17). When he offended many of his contemporaries in Judaism by insisting that feasting, rather than fasting, was to be the rule in the Kingdom of God (Matthew 9:14-17; Mark 2:18-22; Luke 5:33-39), he was announcing the new prophetic era of rejoicing that Zechariah predicted (Zechariah 8:19).

By understanding better where Jesus' teaching came from, and how it derived from the prophetic tradition that fed his vision and encouraged his demand for justice and ethical action, we can also better see where he intended to lead his followers. With the prophets before him, Jesus not only insisted on righteousness from individuals but also wanted communities to live by just judgment. Zechariah summarized centuries of the prophetic imperatives when he said, "Yahweh of armies says this, saying: Judge true judgment, and do mercy and compassion, a man with his brother, and widow and orphan, stranger and poor do not oppress, and do not devise evil, a brother against a man, in your heart" (Zechariah 7:9-10).

In Zechariah's prophecy, as in Jesus' Sermon on the Mount, there is no such thing as requirements for individuals that are separate from human behavior in community. How could there be, when love is at the foundation of the prophetic ethic? That is why, in Zechariah's imperative, Yahweh moves from what the community must do, "Judge true judgment," to what individual Israelites must accomplish, "Do mercy and compassion, a man with his brother." Both parts of this single imperative to righteousness within the Hebrew text appear *in the plural*: Zechariah, like Moses before him and Jesus after him, is addressing his message to people in their totality, living in community and also conscious of themselves as individuals.

The prophetic message does not accept a distinction that has frequently been drawn in the modern phase of Christianity. Since the beginning of the twentieth century, the place of the "Social Gospel" within the faith has been debated. That phrase was introduced in order to call attention to the urgent task of meeting obvious needs in American society on the basis of Jesus' message: at the beginning of the twentieth century, women and children were exploited in the workplace, women could not vote, racism was rife, and monopolies controlled commerce in a way that impoverished many workers. In response to those challenges, Social Gospel teachers such as Walter Rauschenbusch[8] preached that it was the task of believers to reform society in order to exhibit the Kingdom of God within the life of the community.

The idea of social transformation looked increasingly naïve as the twentieth century unfolded, with its wars and economic dislocations. In addition, the growth of Fundamentalism caused many people to think of religion, not in terms of action and conduct, but only as a matter of believing correctly. Both in America and Europe, a divide opened up between those who sought to reform society, whose orientation and methods were increasingly secular, and those who held to a view of faith as a static, unchanging set of beliefs.

Both sides of the divide have suffered from their lack of connection to each other. Social change that ignores or offends the religious sensibilities of a people is difficult to achieve and not likely to last, while any form of religion that insists that only its beliefs are valid and beyond question consigns itself to irrelevance over the long term. Religious fundamentalists, and social reformers who become so antagonistic to religion that they amount to secular fundamentalists, both illustrate a deep defect in the way people conceived of their relationship to one another and to the world as a whole during the twentieth century.

Secular ideologues conceived of human aspirations in such materialist terms that they became unconvincing. Religious ideologues confused their passion for traditional ideas with the living connection that faith seeks to create between believers and God. The prophetic perspective addresses both those problems and heals the rift between social reform and faith that hobbled progress during the twentieth century. Prophecy combines a vision of what God wants for his world with a call to enact that vision.

"The Kingdom of God" is Jesus' name for the connection between what God desires and what people must do. By direct teaching and parable concerning the Kingdom, he spelled out the requirements of justice that any person can fulfill by joining in what God himself is doing in the world. His call to action was neither a matter of people determining their own destiny on their own nor of their passive acceptance of a predetermined plan. Rather, he announced that, just as there are patterns of justice evident on the earth God created, those patterns can be extended into the human world by the way we relate to one another and move together with the power of God.

4
Insight

Mahatma Gandhi used human awareness of our vulnerability to promote social change, applying the Sanskrit conception of Ahimsa, or nonviolence. The content of this teaching helps us understand human identity; the first chapter of *The Way of Jesus*, on Soul, focused on that. Now we investigate a more practical issue concerning Ahimsa: how did Gandhi come to his breakthrough strategy and its application, so that vulnerability in fact became a powerful source of change?

The lineage of his perception is a key to how prophetic actions find appropriate targets and goals by means of insight.

Gandhi forged and explained his teaching of Ahimsa by meditating on the significance of the greatest war poem within the Indian tradition. That he should find Ahimsa in such a source might seem to be a paradox at first sight, but in fact Gandhi's interpretation demonstrates the catalytic capacity of prophetic insight.

When texts are read not simply in their own terms but as maps that guide us in the journey toward relationship with one another and with God, they provide orientation and strategy for what otherwise can easily become aimless wandering. The human journey is always full and exciting, as well as frequently difficult and unnerving, but in all its exhilaration and despondency only insight can weave its disparate parts into purpose.

In the Hindu epic called the *Bhagavad Gita* the sage Krishna explains to the young warrior Arjuna, that—despite his desire to avoid violence—his duty is to go to war. During the course of his explanation, Krishna also reveals his true identity: although he appears to be simply a man of meditation, a Brahmin, he is in fact Brahman itself, the transcendent reality that grounds all things:

> Arjuna, see all the universe,
> animate and inanimate,
> and whatever else you wish to see;
> all stands here as one in my body.[1]

At an immediate level, the *Bhagavad Gita* can be read as compelling support for the absolute necessity of war. After all, as Krishna argues in detail, warfare belongs to the organic whole of the universe.

The requirement to pursue the accomplishment of one's duty in war collides in the *Bhagavad Gita*, as it does in human experience, with the noble human impulse—poignantly expressed by Arjuna—to reject brutality in all its forms.

Arjuna's recoil from battle seems all the more justified and natural because he sees *his own relatives* arrayed for battle opposite him. He is eloquent in his despair, as the bard Sanjaya relates in the *Gita*:

> Dejected, filled with strange pity,
> he said this:
> > Krishna, I see my kinsmen

gathered here, wanting war.
My limbs sink,
my mouth is parched,
my body trembles,
the hair bristles on my flesh.
The magic bow slips
from my hand, my skin burns,
I cannot stand still,
My mind reels.
I see omens of chaos.
Krishna: I see no good
in killing my kinsmen
in battle.
Krishna, I seek no victory,
or kingship or pleasures.
What use to us are kingship,
delights, or life itself?[2]

This war was to be the bloody climax of clan warfare, and Arjuna can see no prospect of a good outcome, whether he wins or loses: "How can we know happiness if we kill our own kinsmen?"

When Krishna explains to Arjuna that duty overrides human emotion, his case for the moral necessity of going to war seems to override compassion:

Death is certain for anyone born,
and birth is certain for the dead;
since the cycle is inevitable,
you have no cause to grieve!
Creatures are unmanifested in origin,
manifest in the midst of life,

and unmanifested again in the end.

Since this is so, why do you lament?[3]

Pressing his argument from death and rebirth to the end, Krishna drives his point home, "Nothing can be better for a warrior than a battle for sacred duty."

Why, then, would Gandhi attempt to explain *from this text* the virtues of Ahimsa, his signature teaching of nonviolence? Part of the answer to that question lies in the standing of the *Bhagavad Gita* within Hinduism, which is a classic from the point of view of its authority—and its popular accessibility. Familiar as the best known epic within the cycle of epics called the *Mahabarata*, the *Gita* is recited and performed at religious festivals and for simple entertainment to this day. From a practical point of view, no religiously grounded argument that did not deal with the *Gita* would be likely to carry the day in India.

At a deeper level, however, Gandhi claimed that Ahimsa was the *ultimate message* of the *Bhagavad Gita*. That was Gandhi's profound contribution to the human art and science of interpretation, and to the inheritance of prophetic insight.

In Gandhi's experience, the *Gita* was not merely one example of the revered Scriptures of Hinduism, but "the mother who never let him down."[4] He read the text regularly, recited it from memory, and appointed it for meditation in his ashrams. To his mind, the battle between clans in the *Gita* does not endorse a literal policy of warfare at all but rather stands for "the war going on in our bodies between the forces of Good (Pandavas) and the forces of Evil (Kauravas)." In his reading, the *Gita* resolves violence instead of promoting violence.

This radical claim is not merely an example of inventive allegory. Gandhi had a total view of the Hindu Scriptures, the Shastras, of which he said all readers need to be aware. His perspective began with the basic, critical distinction between what prophets say on God's behalf and God's own intention. Scriptures, he said, "come through a human prophet, and then through the commentaries of interpreters. None of them comes from God directly."

This perspective, which he also applied to the Gospels, enabled Gandhi to escape a fundamental problem in the Shastras that also challenges a literal reading of the Bible. If we read these sources superficially as the ultimate authority for how to live, we run across the obvious embarrassment that "there is hardly an immoral action for which it would be difficult to find Shastric sanction."

Gandhi addressed this problem directly. He insisted that every reader should engage with the *Bhagavad Gita* on the basis of "something far more powerful than argument, namely, experience." Experience in his understanding went far beyond knowing specific texts or being familiar with a wide range of life's possibilities.

The experience he had in mind was a matter of deep moral feeling. For Gandhi, being human involved sensing how people can learn to live in relationships of justice: "From my youth upwards, I learnt the value of estimating the value of scriptures on the basis of their ethical teaching."

Just as Krishna in the *Gita* speaks of life passing through cycles from the unmanifested, through the manifested, and back to the unmanifested, so Gandhi saw the process of interpretation as moving from the eternal, through the historical words of the Shastras and their interpretation, and into the reader's commitment to eternal principle. "What cannot be followed out in day-to-day practice cannot be called religion."

This understanding of the abiding truth of the Scriptures led Gandhi to use his principle against the conventional understanding of what the *Bhagavad Gita* and other foundational documents of Hinduism truly mean. "Nothing that is inconsistent with the universally accepted first principles of morality has for me the authority of the Shastras." In addition to his successful campaign for Indian independence, Gandhi also exerted sufficient influence so that the caste system of India was abolished in its constitution. His dedication to Ahimsa was not only as a means of attaining a goal, but was also the goal itself.

This ethical program, which Gandhi pursued with learning, dedication, and creative intelligence, was to his mind already embedded in the *Bhagavad Gita*.

In his interpretation, the close of the *Gita*'s second section provided the key to the work as a whole. At that point, Krishna gives strategic guidance for the use of personal discipline in order to overcome the impetus toward useless violence:

> From anger comes confusion;
> from confusion memory lapses;
> from broken memory understanding is lost;
> from loss of understanding, he is ruined.
> But a man of inner strength
> whose senses experience objects
> without attraction and hatred,
> in self-control, finds serenity.

This teaching closes with a clear statement of the aim of this discipline, justifying Gandhi's approach to these lines as expressing Krishna's grounding purpose in the *Bhagavad Gita*:

> This is the place of the infinite Spirit;
> achieving it one is freed of delusion;
> abiding in it even at the time of death,
> one finds the pure calm of eternity.

For Gandhi, the religious value of the *Gita* was that it transcended the occasion of the poem and conveyed the power of discipline to achieve Ahimsa.

Gandhi believed that his reading of the *Bhagavad Gita* was not merely an academic opinion but rather a perspective that grew out of and reinforced his own moral experience—including his own action—as a human being. He accepted that other Hindus in their commentaries showed greater learning than he could boast, and yet insisted, "The *Gita* was not composed as a learned treatise."

The force of his conviction that he lived out a truth of the text, no matter what the incidentals of its articulation, vibrates through his characteristically radical claim, "I believe that the teaching of the *Gita* does not justify war, even if the author of the *Gita* had intended otherwise." Gandhi maintains that the *Bhagavad Gita* expresses a true meaning, a truth that readers and practitioners can and should recognize and enact. As the *Gita's* true meaning is Ahimsa, we should use that standard to correct *both* our own moral actions *and* the understanding of what the *Gita* itself says.

The maneuver Gandhi recommended is not arbitrary, however. Rather, he identified the self-control that produces serenity as the axis of meaning that determines the significance of the entire *Bhagavad Gita* and the whole of human life. Other interpretations of the *Gita* are obviously possible, and Gandhi acknowledged that. He even admitted that he could be mistaken, but if so, "Such a mistake could do no harm either to me or to anybody."

Although Gandhi did not dispute that opinions other than his own were possible and plausible, and that the scholarship of some experts was over his head, he nonetheless saw his dedication to Ahimsa as standing "for unadulterated truth."

In the end, the *Bhagavad Gita* for him was not a historical work at all, but "a great religious book, summing up the truth of all religions." His concern throughout his interpretation was to identify in prophetic fashion the underlying Spirit of the *Gita* within the inheritance of the world's Scriptures, so that he and those who heard his call could incorporate that Spirit within their lives.

In the directness and clarity of his approach, Gandhi reveals important qualities of the interpretation of Scripture by other prophets in very different traditions. For that reason Gandhi's approach illuminates the approach of Jesus.

We saw in the last chapter that, when Jesus spoke of love of God and love of neighbor as summing up the Torah (Matthew 22:34-40; Mark 12:28-34; Luke 10:27-28), the content of his teaching reflected an imperative also voiced in the book of Zechariah (Zechariah 8:16-17), and deeply embedded within the Scriptures of Israel. As in the case of Gandhi, Jesus' genius as a prophet came out less in what he said than in how he arrived at this message, and in how he distilled the wisdom of prophets before him.

The simplest expression of Jesus' principle concerning love appears in Matthew and Mark:

Matthew 22:34-40	Mark 12:28-34
The Pharisees heard that he had shut the Zadokites up, and were gathered together in the same place. And one from them, a lawyer, interrogated him, pressing him to the limit: "Teacher, which decree is great in the law?" But he told him, "You shall love the Lord your God with all your heart and with all your life and with all your mind: the great and first decree is this. A second is like this: You shall love your neighbor as yourself. On these two decrees all the Law is suspended—and the Prophets!"	One of the scribes came forward—hearing them arguing (seeing that he answered them well)—and interrogated him, "Which is the first decree of all?" Jesus answered that: "First is, 'Hear, Israel, our God is the Lord; he is one Lord. And you shall love the Lord your God from all your heart and from all your soul and from all your mind and from all your strength.' This is second: 'You shall love your neighbor as yourself.' There is not another decree greater than these." And the scribe said to him, "Fine, teacher: in truth you have said that he is one and there is not another beside him, and to love him from all heart and from all the understanding and from all the strength and to love the neighbor as oneself is overflowing all burnt offerings and sacrifices." Jesus saw he answered sensibly and said to him, "You are not far from the kingdom of God." And no one any longer dared to interrogate him.

In both Gospels, Jesus is asked by someone outside his group (a Pharisee in Matthew, a scribe in Mark) what is the great (so Matthew) or first (so Mark) commandment. He replies by citing two commandments from the Torah, to love God (drawing from Deuteronomy 6:4, 5) and to love one's neighbor (drawing from a completely different biblical book, Leviticus 19:18).

Jesus concludes in Matthew that all the Law (the Torah) and the Prophets whose works are in the Bible hang from those two commandments, while in Mark he says more simply that there is no other commandment greater than these. In the manner of Gandhi after him in the interpretation of the *Bhagavad Gita*, Jesus did not restrict himself to a single text read only within its own terms of reference. Instead, Jesus seized upon imperatives from different parts of the Torah in order to discover the grounding message of the Bible.

Matthew and Mark make sense of Jesus' teaching somewhat differently, as is only natural, since they were written a generation after the time of Jesus, and each Gospel addresses its own situation in life. In Matthew, the organic connection among the commandments assures that they all hang together (with the teaching of the Prophets) on the principle of love toward God and neighbor (Matthew 22:40). Mark, on the other hand, has the scribe who initiated the scene conclude that to love is more than all burnt offerings and sacrifices (Mark 12:32-33).

The construal of Jesus' teaching in Matthew moves in the direction of claiming that Jesus represents the fulfillment of the Law and the Prophets, a thematic concern of this Gospel in particular. The construal of Jesus' teaching in Mark takes the tack that Jesus' principle establishes a non-ritual means of approval by God, a typically Markan concern.

Both Matthew and Mark find their center of gravity, however, in the conviction that the commandment to love God and love one's neighbor is the action that unites a person with Jesus in an approach to God. The emblem of that approach is fulfillment of the Law and the Prophets in Matthew (22:40), nearness to the Kingdom of God in Mark (12:34). The differences between those construals are not to be minimized: they represent the substantive independence of the Gospels as methods of teaching new believers. But the systemic agreement between Matthew and Mark, that love is the means of access to God after the pattern of Jesus, is an equally striking attribute. The synthesis of the two imperatives, to love God and to love neighbor, into a single principle is Jesus' contribution, a permanent part of our religious inheritance, no matter what one's particular faith or degree of skepticism.

It is a commonplace of academic study to observe that the Jewish teacher Hillel, a near-contemporary of Jesus, is said to have taught—in a dictum comparable to Jesus' teaching—that the Torah is a commentary on the injunction not to do what is hateful to one's neighbor (Bavli, Shabbath 31a). The centrality of the commandment to love one's neighbor is also asserted by Aqiba, the famous rabbi of the second century (Sifra, Leviticus 19:18). Differences of emphasis are detectable and important, but the fact remains that Jesus does not appear to have been exceptional in locating love at the center of the divine commandments. Any rabbi, a teacher in a city or a local village, might have come up with some such principle, although the expressions of the principle attributed to Jesus are especially apt. The principle itself is little more than proverbial: love, after all, is not easily dismissed as a bad idea, or beside the point, and many prophets before Jesus had hammered home their conviction of the necessity of love.

Precisely because the content of Jesus' teaching has clear precedents within the early Judaism of his day, it becomes clear that the tradition presented in aggregate by Matthew and Mark highlights Jesus' originality in explaining the *nature* of the love he demanded of his followers. Jesus' citation of the two biblical passages that demand and define love is for both Matthew and Mark no longer simply a matter of locating a coherent principle within the Torah, in answer to the literal challenge of the question of the Pharisee or scribe. Rather, the twin commandment of love is now held to be a transcendent principle, which fulfills (so Matthew) or supersedes (so Mark) the Torah. Christ himself, by citing and enacting that principle, is held to offer the ethical key to communion with God. Just as Gandhi's teaching of Ahimsa overruled Krishna's defense of war, Jesus' teaching of love overruled the Torah.

Luke's version of the teaching concerning love is quite different from what we find in Matthew and Mark and yet comes by a different route to the same basic message. Luke makes it especially apparent that the significance of Jesus' message lies at least as much in who Jesus is when he speaks as in the exact words that he says (Luke 10:25-37):

> And look, there arose some lawyer, pressing him to the limit, saying, "Teacher, having done what shall I inherit perpetual life?" But he said to him, "In the Law what is written—how do you read?" He answered and said, "You shall love the Lord your God from all your heart and with all your soul and with all your strength and with all your mind, and your neighbor as yourself." Yet he said to him, "You answered rightly: do this,

and you will live." He wanted to justify himself and said to Jesus, "And who is my neighbor?" Jesus took up, and said, "Some person went down from Jerusalem to Jericho, and thugs fell upon him, who stripped him and inflicted lesions. They went away, leaving him half dead. But by coincidence some priest went down that way; he saw him and passed by opposite. Likewise also a Levite came by the place, but he saw and passed by opposite. Some Samaritan made a way and came by him, saw and felt for him. He came forward and, pouring on oil and wine, wrapped his wounds. He mounted him up on his own animal and led him to a hostel and took care of him. On the next day he put out two denarii and gave them to the hosteller and said, Take care of him, and that: Should you spend over, I will repay you when I come back again. Of these three, who seems to you to have become neighbor to the one who fell among the thugs?" Yet he said, "The one who did mercy with him." But Jesus said to him, "Proceed: and you do likewise."

Here an unidentified "lawyer," rather than the Pharisee of Matthew or the scribe of Mark, asks what to do in order to inherit eternal life. In fact, it is not Jesus in Luke who cites the twin principles of love but the lawyer himself (10:27).

At first, Jesus merely confirms what the lawyer already knows (10:28). Jesus' peculiar contribution comes in the response to the lawyer's further question, "Who is my neighbor?" (10:29). The question and the response appear in uniquely Lukan material (10:29-37), the presentation of Jesus' teaching concerning love that was characteristic of the church in Antioch (around the year 90 C.E.) where the Gospel according Luke seems to have been composed.

Luke's expression of the principle of love, in distinction from Matthew's and Mark's, explicitly makes Jesus' *application* of the commandment, rather than its formulation, his systemic innovation. The innovation is effected in the parable of the good Samaritan (Luke 10:29-37). Whether Jesus himself told the parable in just the way Luke presents is beside the present point. What concerns us is that (1) the parable informs the commandment to love with a new emphasis, and that (2) the new emphasis is the systemic center of Lukan ethics, as distinct from Matthean or Markan ethics.

Literally, the parable is designed to answer the question, Who is my neighbor? And that formal issue is also addressed at the close of the parable, when Jesus tells his questioner to go and do what the Samaritan did, that is: show himself a neighbor to someone in obvious need (10:36, 37). But the literal issue in this case is distinct from the underlying issue.

The underlying challenge is not the goodness of the Samaritan, but the fact that he *is* a Samaritan. The victim of the mugging is in no position—in his wounded state—to complain, but especially as a recent pilgrim to Jerusalem, he, as would any Jew, might well have objected to contact with a Samaritan.

Samaritan sacrifice on Mount Gerizim, a practice from the time that the northern region of Israel rebelled against the Davidic monarchy and seceded to form a separate state, was seen as antagonistic to Judaic sacrifice in the Temple on Mount Zion. From the point of view of Judaism, the Samaritans were apostate not only because they rebelled against the house of David but also because their sacrifices on Mount Gerizim included practices from surrounding cultures that violated the Law of Moses.

A priest and a Levite have already passed by in Jesus' parable. The wounded man might have been dead, and the Torah's teaching limited contact with corpses by those involved in serving the Temple (Leviticus 21:1-4). In the parable, then, a victim who *seemed* impure is aided by a Samaritan who *actually was* impure. Nonetheless, Jesus says that the Samaritan's action fulfills the commandment to love one's neighbor as oneself.

The parable of the good Samaritan is a story that formally conveys how to be a neighbor and also how to identify a neighbor. It is shaped systemically to insist that one viewed as "impure" may be a neighbor to one who is "pure." The commandment to love is such that, in its application, it creates a new sphere of purity that transcends any other notion of what is clean and what is unclean.

The issue of purity was crucial to Luke's church in Syrian Antioch. In Galatians 2:11-13, Paul describes factional fighting among three groups in Antioch, the third largest city in the Roman Empire. Their dispute centered on the question of whether Jewish and non-Jewish believers might eat with one another. This was a basic issue of purity that affected not only the common fellowship of Christians but also their practice of the Eucharist.

Paul refers to the factions by naming their leaders. On one extreme, Paul himself taught that Gentiles and Jews might freely eat with one another; on the other, James insisted upon the separation of those who were circumcised Jews from those who were not. Peter and Barnabas were caught somewhere in between.

Much later than Paul, around 90 C.E., Luke's Gospel represents in this parable how the issue was resolved within Christianity in

Antioch. The question of the boundaries established by purity was settled in terms of ethical engagement, rather than dietary practice. It is no accident, then, that it is precisely Luke's Gospel that conveys its unique parable of the good Samaritan, and that its peculiar perspective on how Jesus' teaching regarding love was distinctively concerned with purity.

Jesus provides a paradigm of loving service throughout the literature of the New Testament. The examples that have occupied us so far might easily be multiplied. The link with believers' social situation is so strong in the passages we have considered, *their* lives are mirrored in the situations Jesus is described as confronting. The Gospels are historical, but their historical interest is not only in Jesus but in the challenges those who believed in him confronted decades after the crucifixion.

In the case of both Jesus and the believers, the ethos of the twin commandment of love is transformed by distinctive conditions, so that love might be—for example—the integrating principle of the Torah (Matthew), or a principle beyond cultic Judaism (Mark), or the single term of reference that determines the purity of one person in relation to another (Luke). Prophetic insight permitted the Gospels to apply Jesus' principle of love in new ways, just as it permitted Jesus to discover that principle, and Gandhi to discover Ahimsa in the *Bhagavad Gita*.

Near the end of his life Jesus pursued his own insight further. He taught that every person mirrored God's presence so that even enemies were owed love. God's image was there, shining through the eyes of a neighbor, even if that neighbor hated you. Jesus commanded his followers to love their enemies in unequivocal terms:

Matthew 5:38-48	Luke 6:27-36
You heard that it was said, "Eye for eye and tooth for tooth." Yet I say to you, "Do not resist the evil one, but whoever cuffs you on your right cheek, turn to him the other as well. And to the one who wishes to litigate with you, even to take your tunic, leave him the cloak as well! And whoever requisitions you to journey one mile, depart with him two! Give to the one who asks you, and do not withhold from the one who wishes to borrow from you." You have heard that it was said, "You shall love your neighbor and you shall hate your enemy." Yet I say to you, "Love your enemies, and pray for those who persecute you, so you might become descendants of your father in heavens." Because he makes his sun dawn upon evil people and good people, and makes rain upon just and unjust. For if you love those who love you, what reward have you? Do not even the customs-agents do the same? And if you greet only your fellows, what do you do that goes beyond? Do not even the Gentiles do the same? You, then, shall be perfect, as your heavenly father is perfect.	But I say to you who hear, "Love your enemies, act well with those who hate you, bless those who accurse you, pray concerning those who revile you. To the one who hits you on the cheek, furnish the other also. And from the one who takes your garment, do not forbid the tunic! Give to the one who asks you, and do not demand from the one who takes what is yours. And just as you want men to do to you, do to them similarly. And if you love those who love you, what sort of grace is that for you? Because even the sinners love those who love them. And if you do good to those who do you good, what sort of grace is that to you? Even the sinners do the same. And if you lend to those from whom you hope to receive, what sort of grace is that to you? Even sinners lend so that they receive the equivalent back. Except: love your enemies and do good and lend—anticipating nothing—and your reward will be great, and you will be descendants of most high, because he is fine to the ungrateful and evil. Become compassionate, just as your father is also compassionate."

While arguing with other teachers in Jerusalem, Jesus had come to the realization that the love one owed the Throne of God was exactly what one owed one's neighbor (Mark 12:28-34; Matthew 22:34-40; Luke 10:25-28). Love of God (Deuteronomy 6:5) and love of neighbor (Leviticus 19:18) were basic principles embedded in the Torah, as we have seen. Jesus' innovation lay in the claim that the two were indivisible: love of God *was* love of neighbor, even in the case of enemies, and vice versa.

Every neighbor belonged within God's presence. That is the basis of Jesus' distinctive and challenging ethics of love in the midst of persecution. He linked his ethics to the transformed society the prophets had predicted. His words promise that individual suffering can achieve transcendence, provided the "other" is seen, not as threat or stranger,[5] but as mirroring the presence of God in the world.

Jesus' prophetic style of speech involved him in directly confronting his hearers with what he saw as their lack of comprehension. His severity marks his insistence upon the necessity of discovering insight in order to perceive his distinctive teaching. Jesus even refers to *his own followers* as being hard-hearted, with unseeing eyes and unhearing ears (Mark 8:17-18). This language incorporates the prophecy of Isaiah, particularly in its Aramaic form, the Targum (Targum Isaiah 6:9-10, with innovative material in italics, to indicate additions to the Hebrew text):

> And he said, Go and speak to this people *that* hear *indeed*, but do not understand, and see *indeed*, but do not perceive. Make the heart of this people *dull*, and their ears heavy and their eyes shut; lest *they* see with *their* eyes and hear with *their* ears, and understand with *their* hearts, and repent and *it be forgiven them.*

This Aramaic version of Isaiah, the version that people heard in their own language in synagogue, differed from the Hebrew text. In Hebrew, the prophet is instructed to *tell* the Israelites of his time, "Hear, but do not understand; see but do not perceive." What is in Hebrew a prophetic command is in Aramaic rather a *description* of people who should know better than they do. That is exactly the thought that Jesus delivers to his followers in their common language. His point in alluding to Isaiah 6 is given at the end of the rebuke (Mark 8:21), "Do you not yet understand?"

Jesus' reference to Isaiah 6 in its Targumic form was intended to rouse hearers to understanding, not to cause misunderstanding. This is a case in which Jesus appears to have cited a form of Scripture that is closer to the Targum than to any other extant source; when that happens, an awareness of the fact helps us better understand his preaching.

Targum Isaiah 6:9, 10 is an especially famous example of how Targums can illuminate the Gospels, and it also helps explain Mark 4:11, 12. The statement in Mark could be taken to mean that Jesus told parables with the purpose (*hina* in Greek) that people might see and not perceive, hear and not understand, lest they turn and be forgiven:

> And he was saying to them, "To you the mystery has been given of the kingdom of God, but to those outside, everything comes in parables, so that [*hina*] while seeing they see and do not perceive, and while hearing they hear and do not understand, lest they repent and it be forgiven them."

The Targum also (unlike the Hebrew text) refers to people not being "forgiven" (rather than not being "healed"), and that suggests that the Targum may give the key to the meaning presupposed by Jesus.

The relevant clause in the Targum refers to people who behave *in such a way* —"so that" (the simple letter *d* [daleth] in Aramaic)— they see and do not perceive, hear and do not understand, lest they repent and they be forgiven. It appears that Jesus was characterizing people in the Targumic manner, just as he characterized his own fate similarly in Mark with a clause employing *hina* (cf. 9:12); he was not acting in order to be misunderstood.

In this famous case from Mark,[6] then, the underlying Aramaism of using the clause with *d* caused the saying of Jesus to use the term *hina* in Greek, which may mean "in order that" or "so that." With the former meaning, Mark's Jesus speaks so as not to be understood, and deliberately to preclude the forgiveness of those who do not understand. With the latter meaning, Jesus referred to Isaiah in its Targumic form in order to characterize the *kind* of people who do not respond to his message and what happens to them. The fact of the similarity in wording with the Targum shows us that the second meaning is much more likely.

Prophetic insight in Jesus' teaching emerges not only when Scriptures are literally cited, as in the case of his perspective on the commands to love God and love neighbor, but also when he applied scriptural language (such as from the Aramaic version of Isaiah 6) directly to his hearers. To his mind, the same Spirit that was active in prophecy was also present in the experience of those around him. Scripture was indeed being fulfilled by means of insight.

In the Gospel according to John, Jesus' insight is conveyed by a narrative that occurs early in the text (John 1:43-50). At first, this story seems cryptic, but it illustrates prophetic insight when it is read in terms of the Scriptures it relates to.

In John's Gospel, Jesus calls Philip to be a disciple. Philip then tells his brother Nathanael, "We have found the one concerning whom Moses and the Prophets wrote." Nathanael, from the cosmopolitan city of Bethsaida, is skeptical about a rabbi from a negligible Galilean hamlet on the other side of the Sea of Galilee. He says, "Can anything good be from Nazareth?" Yet his doubt is overcome when Jesus tells him, "Before Philip called you, I saw you under the fig tree." That changes Nathanael's mind about Jesus.

Indeed, Nathanael's enthusiasm might seem to be exaggerated, until the underlying scriptural prophecy in Jesus' statement is identified. Nathanael says, "Rabbi, you are the Son of God, you are the king of Israel!" Why this radical change of attitude?

The prophetic image of every Israelite living under his own vine and his own fig tree symbolized the prosperity God intended for his people, and was articulated by several of the Prophets (Micah 4:4; Zechariah 3:10, see also Isaiah 36:16; 1 Kings 4:25). The point of the image was that Israel would not merely survive with necessities such as grain and water, but also—above and beyond survival—would enjoy the products of vine and fig for celebration and sweetness, enjoyment well beyond subsistence.

Nathanael, who was a "true Israelite" according to Jesus, belonged in that picture of prophetic promise. When Nathanael embraced Jesus' insight, it was because Jesus had placed Nathanael within the messianic vision of Israel as a whole. The ancient prophetic promise, Jesus said, was something Nathanael would realize as a matter of experience.

Yet just as Jesus could banter with his disciples using prophetic language, accusing them of having eyes and not seeing, so also he goads Nathanael, "Because I said to you that I saw you under the fig tree, do you believe? Greater things than these shall you see."

Jesus then says what these "greater things" are, again using a prophetic image (John 1:51):

> You shall see heaven opened, and the angels of God ascending and descending on the Son of Man.

As in the case of several of Jesus' teachings, only someone familiar with biblical imagery can understand him. Here, Jesus alludes to the story of Jacob's dream at Bethel, when the patriarch saw the angels of God ascending and descending by a ladder leading to heaven (Genesis 28:10-22).

Jacob's alternative name was Israel, so that Jesus makes the connection between Israelites such as Nathanael and their eponymous patriarch. In addition, the point of the angelic dream in Genesis is the fulfillment of promise: "I will not leave you until I have done what I have promised you" (Genesis 28:15). Just as Jesus saw Nathanael under the fig tree of messianic promise, so he implied that Nathanael would see the same kind of fulfilment of the prophecy that Jacob enjoyed.

In the way of other prophets before him, some of Jesus' images depend upon the language in which he originally spoke. The term "Son of Man" (*bar nasha'* in Aramaic) is a case in point. The phrase can mean both a particular human being and also *any* human being in the situation described. Jacob's dream in Genesis presented a ladder as the conduit between heaven and earth; in Jesus' prophecy, a person, "the Son of Man," replaces the ladder. Following the meaning of that phrase in Aramaic, Jesus was saying that he himself, Nathanael, and anyone with eyes to see could become the link between this world and the promises of God.

Jesus obviously explained himself in much less detail than Mahatma Gandhi. In fact, part of this method of teaching seems to have been to skimp on explanation in order to jar those who heard him into insight. That is also a part of the prophetic pattern. But from Isaiah and Micah during the eighth century B.C.E., through Jesus, and on to Gandhi in recent times, the basic axis of prophetic insight has run from sacred texts, through the interpretation of what the divine will truly is, and into human action in the present.

5
Forgiveness

Jesus' few short years in the fishing village of Capernaum, by the Sea of Galilee, gave him the most settled period of his adult life. He lived in the household of two brothers and their families, Simon and Andrew. He became a virtual member of their extended family as his reputation as a rabbi grew. This time of relative calm, and of his careful nurture of his disciples and their development, resulted in Jesus' insight that healing could be produced as a result of forgiveness.

The story of the healing of Simon Peter's mother-in-law from a fever (Matthew 8:14-15; Mark 1:29-31; Luke 4:38-39) derives from this time. Mark's Gospel, the earliest account, describes the woman as "prone, fevered," when the disciples speak to Jesus about her. There was no such thing as a slight fever during the first century. Influenza and infections could kill and often did, especially the young and the old.

Yet Jesus seems almost casual; his treatment of the woman is uncomplicated (Mark 1:31): "He came forward and raised her—grasping the hand. And the fever left her, and she was providing for them." "Providing for" Jesus' friends and followers meant preparing food in the short term, and cooking, cleaning, and gardening for them on a regular basis. She simply took up her life where she had left it off.

This early account of Jesus' healing in the Gospel according to Mark puts an emphasis on touch. He grasps the fevered woman's hand, and that contact releases her from her sickness. How Jesus understood release to occur is not yet explained (although Mark does give us the explanation in the next chapter of the Gospel, as we will come to). For the moment, Mark foregrounds the fact of physical touch as the medium of healing, as is characteristic of this Gospel.

In another episode Jesus spits on his fingers, sticking them into a deaf mute's ears and mouth, grabbing his tongue and saying in Aramaic, "*Ephphatha* [that is, Be opened up]" (Mark 7:34). In the following chapter of Mark, Jesus spits right into a blind man's eyes and lays hands on them in a healing which takes two treatments to be effective (Mark 8:22-26). From the earliest commentators to this day, Mark's graphic portrayal of Jesus' physical manipulations during the course of healing have been described as being disturbing and crude. But in Jesus' mind they served a precise purpose.

The tactile focusing of Jesus' power of healing by means of physical contact and manipulation is diminished in the other Gospels of the New Testament, which were written later than Mark. As time went on, Christians portrayed Jesus' activity as more and more logocentric: he just speaks, and healing happens spontaneously (see, for example, Matthew 8:16). As Christianity took on an increasingly Hellenistic character, its portraits of Jesus became more philosophical, sometimes to the point of making him seem remote from other people. He no longer spat or grabbed at hands and tongues. The earthiness of his rabbinic persona was covered over with a patina of omniscient reserve.

Widespread healing in and around Capernaum (Mark 1:39; Matthew 8:16; Luke 4:40-41) punctuated Jesus' teaching. His genuine fame as a healer bolstered his confidence as a rabbi, so that the number of his disciples grew. He instructed them in his own method of healing, and eventually sent some of *them* (Mark 6:13) to anoint the sick with oil in order to offer healing in the way he did.

Among all of Jesus' disciples, Mary Magdalene was the most famous anointer, and it is appropriate that a woman should have been known in that role, since anointing was understood as part of a woman's work in Jewish antiquity.[1] But Jesus generalized anointing (Mark 6:13), and therefore physical contact, as a signature activity of all his disciples, men as well as women.

As Jesus' fame as a healer grew, the quiet solitude of the wilderness became a necessary relief from his contact with those who sought his help. He needed to replenish himself, and to teach those closest to him in a place where they could concentrate on the mysteries of the Kingdom and take up the activity of healing themselves. These retreats offered a respite from the excesses that Capernaum offered, as well as from the busy household routines of work and social life and family responsibilities that cut into Jesus' meditative discipline.

Desperate crowds that clamored for his healing disturbed him to the point that he would pick up a few belongings and leave Capernaum for days (Mark 1:35-37):

> Very—at night—early, he arose and went away into a wilderness place, and there he was praying. And Simon and those with him pursued him, and found him and said to him that All are seeking you.

These retreats were sporadic and short-lived, but they punctuated Jesus' movements in and around Capernaum.

The crush of those who sought cures sometimes became dangerous, and chaos frequently swirled around Jesus in Capernaum. The pressure on him there was sometimes acute. He sought relief from travel in wilderness areas (Mark 1:35; Luke 4:42), camping for days at a time, usually alone, but often with eager disciples and would-be devotees (Mark 1:36; Luke 4:42).

Capernaum was his base during this period, but even the protection of Simon and Andrew's courtyard complex was no match for the crowds who were desperate for the healing purity of Jesus' touch. For many people in Galilee, as in Jesus' vision at his baptism, the heavens were splitting open and the Spirit was available to God's chosen people in this rabbi who seemed to have almost limitless power as he walked the roads near the Sea of Galilee.

In one particular story (Mark 2:1-12; Matthew 9:1-8; Luke 5:17-26), the detail of the narrative of how crowds could press in on Jesus results in the disclosure of precisely how Jesus understood that his power of healing worked. When he had returned to his base in Capernaum after a brief retreat into the wilderness, he was teaching in a small house where a paralyzed man was brought to him.

Those who carried the man were prevented from getting to Jesus by the crowd that thronged around the house, for whom each healing was a new eruption of Spirit, a step toward the Kingdom of God. The man's bearers actually had to dig through the earthen roof and lower him to Jesus on his litter. "Your sins are released," Jesus said, and the man walked.

By this time Jesus had already been acknowledged in Galilee as a rabbi: a master of Israelite tradition whose actions were equal to his words. His teaching had made him seem like some other Galilean rabbis, who were known as *chasidim*. During the Maccabean revolt that followed the desecration of the Temple in 167 B.C.E., the term *chasidim* was applied to Jews who were so faithful to the Torah that they preferred to die rather than to do violence on the Sabbath (see 1 Maccabees 2:29-48). Having known the *chesed*, the compassion of God, they refused to betray their compassionate Lord.

That sense of the integrity involved in being a *chasid* carried on long after the Maccabees. By the first century, however, the word applied especially to rabbis who were shown to have obtained divine compassion, not only for themselves, but also on behalf of others. These rabbis cured sickness and relieved drought through prayer: that was the mark of divine compassion working through them.

To understand Jesus and other *chasidim*, we must enter into the mindset of a world in which God's power was known to transform people physically, not only ethically and spiritually. *Chasidim* differed considerably on *how* divine mercy was accessed and divine healing occurred, but they insisted *that* God's power, when accessed, could overwhelm any illness.

One famous *chasid*, named Chanina ben Dosa, a later-first-century rabbi from Jesus' region of Galilee, said healing stemmed from the fluency of his prayer. Chanina lived only ten miles from Nazareth, in a village called Arav.

Chanina was so famous, a leader of the Pharisees in Jerusalem named Gamaliel[2] once sent two of his students all the way up to Galilee to have Chanina pray for Gamaliel's son, who was ill. Chanina told the envoys that the fever had departed. They asked him, "Are you a prophet?" He replied: "I am no prophet, nor a prophet's son, but this is how I am favored. If my prayer is fluent in my mouth, I know one is favored; if not, I know the illness is fatal." When the emissaries returned to Jerusalem, Gamaliel reported to them that the fever had left his son at exactly the time Chanina had spoken (Berakoth 34b in the Babylonian Talmud).[3]

Here indeed was a *chasid*, obtaining mercy on behalf of others. Confidence that a *chasid*'s claim on divine compassion could work at a distance is also reflected in a famous story about Jesus (John 4:43-53). But *chasid*s were not all alike, and every rabbi had his own characteristic view of both his teaching and his practice.

Jesus identified forgiveness, rather than prayer, as the means by which God produced healing. "Your sins are released," became his characteristic declaration to those who were healed by his touch; his typical advice after a healing, "sin no more," was complementary to that.

A haunting story in the Gospel according to Luke, regarding a sinful woman misidentified as Mary Magdalene in later Christian tradition,[4] brings out the relationship between these expressions clearly. In this anointing story, a Pharisee named Simon hosts a meal for Jesus in Capernaum (Luke 7:36-50). The whole scene runs counter to the bias against Pharisees in the Gospels, proving that not all Pharisees were Jesus' enemies. Many of them respected him and were curious about his teaching; some even welcomed him into their homes.

Simon must have been wealthy, perhaps a merchant in olive oil from Galilee, which was treasured by Jews as far away as Syria for its quality and because it was *kosher*.[5] The Pharisee's house would have been large and well appointed, but without the decadent, Hellenistic opulence of the homes in Capernaum, whose citizens' ostentatious wealth Jesus criticized.

By inviting Jesus into his home, Simon also opened his doors to Jesus' disciples, followers, and others who came to listen to the rabbi and sit with him out of simple curiosity. One of the curious was a woman described in Luke as "sinful." When she saw Jesus and heard him speak, she cast herself at his feet, repenting of her sins. She wept and "began with tears to wet his feet and with the hair of her head she wiped and kissed his feet and anointed with ointment" (Luke 7:38). Her act doubtless silenced the chattering, rambunctious crowd. His feet would have been filthy from Capernaum's streets—and the washing of his feet with her hair and tears remains a beautiful, haunting image.

Legends developed after the time of the New Testament have portrayed her as a prostitute, but there is no evidence of that. The fact that the woman is simply called "sinful," without explanation, conceivably intimates that she had been known somehow for sexual impropriety. But there are many, many sins that do not involve sex. In any case, even in cases where women were blamed for their sexual conduct, prostitution was often not at issue. Perhaps the woman in Luke had gone through a series of spouses the way the Samaritan woman did (see John 4:5-42). Another possibility is that she had flouted the rules that sought to govern whether an Israelite from one social group could marry someone from a different group.[6] Given the elegant gesture with her hair, it is more likely she pursued the forbidden profession of a hairdresser, which many rabbis saw as just a step away from prostitution, since touching in private or semi-private was involved.

The Pharisee was offended that Jesus accepted the touch of a recognized sinner, but Jesus pronounced that her sins had been forgiven, articulating one of his core principles (Luke 7:47): "Her many sins have been released, because she loved much: but to whom little is released, loves little." Those who are unaware of how much they have been forgiven love only a little. By contrast, those who consciously accept divine forgiveness, which releases them from their self-imposed shackles, are alive to the bounty that comes from God alone and are willing to extend that forgiving power to others, in generous, spontaneous acts like the hairdresser's. Her lavish embrace of Jesus was itself an extension of divine compassion, proof that she had been taken up and purified by God's love.

Jesus openly says to the woman, not only that her sins are released (Luke 7: 48), but also: "Your faith has saved you. Depart in peace" (Luke 7:50). Being forgiven requires not only the power of God; in addition, human trust[7] in God's capacity and will to forgive must be present. Once present, forgiveness occurs, and one is sent on the way of wholeness, the basic sense of the term "peace" (*shalom*) in Semitic languages.

Jesus' language of forgiveness reflects the Judaic view of sin as restriction, a binding of one's natural capacity. The grounding conception is that wrong actions produce damaging consequences. A thief, for example, imposes a shackle on his victim and on himself. A person who has been robbed remains fearful, suspicious, and often profoundly insecure long after the theft. And the thief shackles him or herself to an identity that is unproductive, reliant on deception—and often increasingly violent. Both the perpetrator and the victim find their natural capabilities and responses inhibited—and sometimes crippled—by the fact of the theft.

One of the most insidious features of sin is that it impinges on *anyone* associated with the wrong, not only with the person or persons responsible. The prophets Jeremiah and Ezekiel foresaw a different order altogether (Jeremiah 31:29-30; cf. Ezekiel 18:2):

> In those days they will no longer say, "The fathers eat sour grapes
> and the sons' teeth are set on edge." But each will die for his own
> iniquity—a man who eats sour grapes, his teeth shall be set on
> edge.

The result of sin would at last be limited, in their prophetic vision.

Jesus takes the vision of Jeremiah and Ezekiel a step further. The
issue as he saw it was not *who* sinned at all but dealing directly
with the *results* of sin. His perspective comes to poetic expression
in the Gospel according to John (John 9:2-3):

> And his disciples questioned him, saying, "Rabbi, who sinned,
> this man or his parents, that he was born blind?" Jesus answered,
> "Neither he nor his parents sinned, but in order that the works of
> God might be manifested in him."

The origin of the sin was inconsequential, compared to the possibility that God's glory could be revealed by overcoming sin.

The way to break free of a shackle or bond is to release it. To
release sin—and "release" is what the terms in Greek, Hebrew, and
Aramaic (*luo* and *shabaq*) that are traditionally rendered as "forgive" actually mean—was therefore God's purpose. This was how
the man in Mark who was crippled was healed according to Jesus;
his legs and his sins were unbound. The current, weakened conception of forgiveness as merely overlooking or forgetting the
harm one has suffered is a far cry from the Judaic sense of liberation from the consequences of one's own deeds and the deeds of
others. Jesus was not interested in politely trying to ignore wrong
actions: he wanted to confront wrong and to free people from the
harm that wrong can do.

A story comparable to Mark's paralytic in the Gospel according
John is set at Bethesda in Jerusalem. When Jesus tells the healed

man to sin no more (John 5:14), he affirms that divine release from sin produces health, and that one's health depends upon that awareness. For Jesus, the meaning of wholeness was release from sin and the sense of full integrity as an Israelite that come from being forgiven. Healing followed naturally. In a culture in which sins were understood to be binding constraints, and demons could lay siege to any part of the human body, it was natural for illness to be manifested by a person feeling enfeebled, unable to move.

The common experience of being weak, not quite in one's own body, was diagnosed as being alienated by God. Immobility signaled both disease and its underlying cause. There was no rigid separation between body and mind in this ancient worldview. Both were ruled by spirits, whether harmful or healing, which exerted their influence, producing times of sickness and health, sin and forgiveness, paralysis and ecstasy.

But there was also a profoundly challenging side to Jesus' chasidic teaching on forgiveness. Towns such as Capernaum conducted a brisk trade with Romans, non-Jewish Syrians, and Galileans—anyone who was fond of salted fish. Their wealth, while not comparable to Jerusalem's, was unlike what Jesus was familiar with in the hillsides of Lower Galilee. Here was a Galilee committed to currency rather than the exchange of goods and services, to *mammon*—as Jesus derisively called money in his native Aramaic (Luke 16:13), using a term that implied bribery—rather than the produce of God's own land.

Jesus reacted fiercely to the relative sophistication of Capernaum's economy, in a way that tied together God's willingness to forgiveness with people's capacity to let go of a stringent accounting of what was owed to them. As a rural Galilean Jew, Jesus distrusted and even detested money. He regaled his dinner companions by lampooning the attitude of the self-important materialists of thriving little ports like Capernaum's.

The most notorious case of his negative reaction to a conventional reckoning of wealth has long perplexed commentators (Luke 16:1-9):

> Yet he was saying to the students, "There was some rich person who had an administrator, and he was denounced to him as squandering his belongings. He called him and said to him, 'What is this I hear about you? Render the account of your administration, because you are not able to administer still!' The administrator said within himself, *What shall I do? Because my lord will remove the administration from me! I am not capable of digging, and ashamed to beg. I know what I shall do! So that when I am displaced from the administration, they might take me into their own houses.* He summoned each one of the indebted of his own lord and was saying to the first, 'How much do you owe my lord?' Yet he said, 'A hundred *baths* of oil.' But he said to him, 'Take your bills and sit: quickly write fifty!' Accordingly, he said to another, 'But you owe how much?' Yet he said, 'A hundred *kors* of wheat.' He says, 'Take your bills and write eighty!' And the lord praised the administrator for the injustice—because he had acted cleverly, for the sons of this epoch are cleverer than the sons of light among their own generation. And I say to you, Make yourselves friends from the *mammon* of injustice, so that when it fades they will take you into perpetual shelters."

How can Jesus have advocated corrupt behavior? For Jesus the Galilean rabbi, money really is *"mammon* of injustice," corrupt currency; it might as well be used to buy the friendship within Israel that really counts. His depiction of the ambiance of dishonesty in what the Romans would call a *latifundium* (an absentee landlord's estate) is as exaggerated as his picture of the amounts due, represent many times what an ordinary farm could produce in a year.

The lord praised the steward for his cleverness (v. 8) in reducing the debts of those who owed commodities to the lord (vv. 5-7). The scheme was devised so that the lucky debtors would receive the steward (v. 4) after his lord had followed through on the threat of dismissing the steward for dishonesty (vv. 1-2). On any ordinarily moral accounting, the steward had gone from bad to worse, and yet his lord praises him (v. 8). Because God is the lord, what would be bribery in the case of any ordinary master's property turns out to be purposeful generosity. The effect of the steward's panic is to fulfill the lord's desire.[8] Profit, in Jesus' provincial understanding, was a chimera that was unworthy of human effort; in his Galilean vision of fertility and exchange, commerce was a blight.

Back in Nazareth, everyone was in debt. That is why Jesus and countless other Jews referred to sin as "debt" in the Aramaic language of both Judea and Galilee. This widespread use of the term "debt" (*chova'*) to mean a sin before God points to the extent to which indebtedness had become endemic. Peasants owed owners of the *latifundia* a rent in currency that they could not pay; year by year, they handed over the rich produce of their harvests just to be allowed to remain indentured on their land, owing more and more *mammon* they did not have. The burden of owing what could not be repaid became the principal metaphor of that alienation from God for which one prayed for release.

When Jesus spoke of forgiveness, he spoke from that cultural context. "Debt" was so overwhelming there was no question of paying if off: it had to be wiped out. Like the manager in the parable, only those who were willing to forgive the debts of others truly understood the key to their own forgiveness.

Jesus looked at Capernaum through the suspicious eyes of an outsider, shocked at the prominent display of debt-acquired wealth. The relative wealth of these towns, precisely because they were Jewish, offended him and many other Galilean peasants. The residents proudly built synagogues, but their efforts in Jesus' eyes were useless for the simple reason that "you can not serve God and mammon" (Luke 16:13; Matthew 6:24), any more than you can both ask God for release from your debts and demand payment on the debts that others owe you.

Jesus took particular aim at the banquets of the wealthy Jews, financed by debt, which stood in sharp contrast to the informal celebration of his meals with his disciples and sympathizers. Capernaum's banquets were elaborate Graeco-Roman symposia, sometimes involving a special room in a large house to accommodate guests who lounged on scrolled oak couches, gleaming with walnut oil worked into the rich grain of the wood. The couches were covered with linen blankets and pillows of crimson, indigo, and a spectrum of greens and yellows, and embroidered with Syrian images of birds and trees. Orange dye for the cloth was made from henna, red from safflowers, yellow from saffron, purple from expensive murex snails from Phoenicia. Ornate end tables set beside a couch assured that its sole use would be for the serious business of lounging. The richest merchants displayed their wealth with columned halls and floors with mosaic tile work formed into abstract motifs. To Jesus, and to many rabbis and other Jews like him, such dwellings were a travesty. What were they doing in Jewish Galilee?

These elaborate Jewish households catered to local dignitaries, the wealthier businessmen in the community who controlled fishing fleets, fish-salting, and the transport of their Galilean product by pack animals and carts drawn by oxen. Every business transaction in ancient Palestine needed to be sanctioned by both the Roman tax collector and the centurion responsible for order and security in his area. The tax agent (*telones* in Greek) was a private contractor who bid for the position of serving as Rome's agent (with a commission). The level of tax he imposed on transactions could be sweetened by bribery and lavish entertainment. A centurion, similarly, was always alert for ways to supplement his income and enliven his austere routine. He needed an incentive to permit Jewish caravans to arm themselves and even more encouragement to agree to provide an armed guard himself.

When a valuable caravan set out, mounted riders armed with short swords and javelins were either provided by the local garrison, or the garrison-commander sanctioned the employment of mercenaries. Symposia were ideal occasions for currying favor with local authorities, however much they clashed with the ethos of Judaism and abrogated the commandments of Moses.

Rich foreign clients, principal customers of Galilean fish from around Galilee itself, Syria (including what is now Lebanon), and Decapolis, regaled themselves at these banquets. Professional musicians of both sexes entertained with flute and lyre; they also doubled as acrobats and danced, their skills deployed to delight and divert.

The host's object at a banquet was to draw the best, most influential guests, whether Jewish or not, just as the intention of guests was to be treated with the greatest possible honor. Jesus' response to these banquets was trenchant and categorical: invite the indigent; prefer the lowest places (Luke 14:7-14). In short, abhor the depraved celebration of status in the symposia that infected Capernaum. The decadence of the town disgusted him. When it came to his meals with followers, Jesus was proud to be called, not a symposial host, but—as he himself cited, as had adversaries—"a glutton and a drunkard, a friend of customs-agents and sinners" (Luke 7:35; Matthew 11:19). His purpose was not to impress or to curry favor but to encounter sinners as sinners, both in need of forgiveness and prepared to extend that release to others. "The merciful are favored," he said (Matthew 5:7), "because they will receive mercy."

Jesus pressed his case relentlessly for the necessity of forgiveness by means of the metaphorical language of release and debt, but no one explained more passionately or more existentially than Paul of Tarsus how powerful forgiveness could be.[9] His realization that Christ had appeared to him, raised from the dead, while he was on the way to Damascus in order to *persecute* followers of Jesus, transformed him.

If God could embrace him in this way, Paul taught, despite his resistance, then God's compassion had to radiate from Paul himself to others: "Everything comes from God, who reconciled us to himself through Christ and gave to us the ministry of reconciliation" (2 Corinthians 5:18). To Paul's mind, forgiveness amounted to a fresh creative act from God (2 Corinthians 5:17), "So that: if any is in Christ, he is a new creation; the old has passed, look—the new has become."

The moment of this disclosure of God's compassion, which Paul typically referred to as "grace" (*kharis* in Greek, a term that often renders *chesed* in the Greek translation of the Hebrew Scriptures), gave people who had known forgiveness the commission to mediate forgiveness to others.

Paul spoke of his own existential moment of new creation as "When it pleased the one who separated me from my mother's belly and called me through his grace to uncover his Son in me so that I should announce him triumphant among the Gentiles" (Galatians 1:15-16). This revelation was prophetic—like a prophet, Paul felt he had been predestined to this moment from his "mother's belly" (a phrase that appears in Jeremiah 1:5 and Isaiah 49:1-6). The unveiling of God's Son within took priority over any human contact or circumstance, and Paul does not even speak of his own baptism at this point in his Letter to the Galatians (although the book of Acts does).

Paul puts the deep content of this experience so economically that its pivotal reference has been missed by some commentators: God determined "to uncover his Son in" Paul. Conventional translations have stood in the way of what he clearly said here. The term "uncover" (*apokalupsai*) in Greek is typically rendered "reveal" in English versions of the Bible. By the same token, the noun *apokalupsis*, our word "apocalypse," becomes "revelation." These translations make readers think in terms of external stimuli coming to the seer like ordinary sense perceptions. The basic meaning of these Greek terms, however, is that a heavenly mystery has its cover (its *-kalupsis*) taken off (*apo*): the veil of circumstance is momentarily stripped from spiritual reality. Here the cover is removed from God's Son, who is "in" (*en*) Paul, within his consciousness in an experience uniquely his.

Paul's experience was not of an external event that other people witnessed with him. He alone was converted that day. His companions are described in the book of Acts as confused, and Acts emphasizes their confusion by describing their experience in contradictory ways: did they hear something and see nothing (so

Acts 9:7) or the reverse (so Acts 22:9)? Paul's reference in Galatians relates to a personal moment of disclosure, an unveiling of the divine. Paul calls what was disclosed within him God's "Son."

Readers today think exclusively of Jesus when they hear the words the "Son of God." But the phrase had a life of its own before it was applied to Jesus, as we saw in chapter 2, referring to angels (Genesis 6:2), the whole people called Israel (Hosea 11:1), and the king in David's line (Psalm 2:7). Direct revelation extends God's favor to people and angels; each is "the Son," "the beloved," as Jesus became in his vision at his baptism (Mark 1:11).

Baptism, in fact, was when, according to Paul, God sends the Spirit of his Son into every believer, who cries to God, "Abba, Father" (Galatians 4:6). The believer becomes a Son, just as Jesus called upon his father; as Paul says in the same sentence, God sends his Spirit "because you are Sons." The moment of baptism, the supreme moment of faith, was when one discovered oneself as a Son of God, because Jesus as God's Son was disclosed in one's heart.

When Paul felt the divine Son uncovered within himself, he encountered the divine presence he had sought for in the Temple, but now it was available inside him. Because he knew he was in the presence of the divine during his experience on the road to Damascus, the answer to the urgent question he asked, "Who are you, Lord?" came as the most terrifying thing he ever heard. "I am Jesus, whom you persecute!" (Acts 26:15). No response could have agonized him more. Profound loyalty to the Temple, not malice, had led Paul to serve Caiaphas, to resist the malcontents from Galilee and the Diaspora who claimed their dead rabbi's authority superseded the high priest's. Yet now this angel-like Son of God identified himself as Jesus, risen from the dead.

That ended Paul's commission as a Pharisee in the service of Caiaphas, and in his own mind it also put him irrevocably in the wrong. God revealed his Son in Paul, but as an accuser. Biographers and others have remarked on the guilt that Paul's letters sometimes express, but looking for mysterious psychological causes is superfluous. He openly admitted (1 Corinthians 15:9): "I am the least of the apostles who is not worthy to be called an apostle, since I persecuted the church of God." He not only acknowledged his guilt in so many words but also spoke of it while referring to Jesus' resurrection and the experience of the divine Son's appearance that made him an apostle.

While traveling to Damascus, vision taught Paul that the Galilean rabbi whose movement he had been trying to stamp out was God's Son. There really is no mystery about the source of Paul's sense of guilt.

This painful dissonance, between knowing the divine Son within him and a profound conviction of his unworthiness, never left Paul. That tension powered his ceaseless activity: he might not be worthy to be called an apostle, "but I labored more than all of them" (1 Corinthians 15:10). He strove to work off his unintended blasphemy against God's Son, turning his life over to the guidance of prophetic vision. This divine Son could become the holy, divine center within every person, as Jesus had become within Paul: Paul's vision gave him the theme of his thought, and of his life.

Paul believed God disclosed the divine Son within him for a specific purpose: "So that I should announce him triumphant among the Gentiles" (Galatians 1:16). In Acts as well, the risen Jesus gives him a new commission to replace the one he had accepted from Caiaphas (Acts 26:18): to go to Gentiles, "to open their eyes, to turn from darkness to light, and from the power of Satan unto God, so they receive forgiveness of sins." By working out divine forgiveness among Gentiles, Paul pursued the forgiveness he needed personally.

Paul's vision was not—and could not have been—one of personal acceptance by God. He had persecuted the same divine Son now unveiled within him. Even toward the end of his life, beset by the machinations of the Roman legal system, he acknowledged that his inner insecurity was greater than any exterior threat. He actively courted suffering in imitation of Jesus (Philippians 3:10-11) "that somehow I might attain to the resurrection from the dead." Paul never doubted the reality of his vision, but—in a way that later influenced Augustine and Calvin—he was never sure he really could be part of such glory.

To Paul's mind, his sin against the risen Jesus was so great that he could no more count on salvation than Gentiles could. His struggle for their forgiveness was concurrently a struggle for his own.

Paul says with unmistakable emphasis, then, that God chose "to uncover his Son in me so that I should announce him triumphant among the Gentiles." *His* deliverance by the realization of the Son within implied that *they* could be delivered the same way in an outbreak of unprecedented redemption. That is why his conversion involved both a personal conviction of his guilt and a commission to announce Christ to non-Jews. In their forgiveness, their sanctity, he sought the assurance of his own. Paul's acknowledgment of guilt and his quest for forgiveness proved to be profoundly creative forces.

Sonship, forgiveness, God imparting Spirit are all visionary realities that Paul encountered in Jesus, risen from the dead. They amounted to seeing God making humanity anew. The task his conversion to Jesus gave him was to mediate this same Spirit to all people who were prepared to receive the Christ in faith. God had started making Paul a new person in the uncovering of the divine Son within him, and he set about making new people in this image, Gentiles included.

How is it that Paul's insecurity and sense of guilt became a creative force, rather than a crippling inhibition? He explained that himself, writing in his Letter to the Romans, "For I am not ashamed of the message, because it is God's power for salvation to all who believe, to Jew first and to Greek. Because God's righteousness is disclosed in him from faith to faith, just as it is written, the righteous one from faith shall live" (Romans 1:16-17). Paul took evocative words from the book of Habakkuk, "the righteous one from faith shall live" (Habakkuk 2:4) and gave them new meaning.

Faith, in Paul's understanding, was the basis on which a human being could stand in relation to God, acknowledging sin, but also laying claim to the grace of God. Faith was the willingness to reflect back to God the compassion God had shown by means of forgiveness. Calling God "Abba" was not only an acknowledgment that God established a new relationship by forgiving a sinner but that the sinner embraced the intimacy of that new relationship as a principal orientation within life.

The force of this new relationship is also visible in its dark side. Paul spoke of deliberately *withdrawing* the possibility of forgiveness from a person, when he wrote his First Letter to the Corinthians. Having chided congregations for their factionalism, he asked them with studied majesty: "What do you want? Shall I come to you with a rod, or in love, in a spirit of gentleness?" (1 Corinthians 4:21). That "rod" was a matter of the force he could exert, and not only when present personally. First Corinthians shows precisely how Paul thought his authority could be brought to bear in his absence.

Paul was angry to his core about some behavior in Corinth. A man there was sleeping with a woman who had been his father's wife (1 Corinthians 5:1). This was off the chart of permissible behavior even "among the Gentiles," and violated Paul's principle that everyone should "keep one's own vessel in sanctification and honor, and not in the passion of lust just like the Gentiles who do not know God" (1 Thessalonians 4:4-5).

But what he then says goes beyond anger. Paul judges the Corinthians *in absentia* (1 Corinthians 5:3-5):

> For absent in body but present in the Spirit, I have already judged—as being present—the man who has behaved this way. In the name of our Lord Jesus, when you have gathered and my spirit is with the power of our Lord Jesus—turn over such a man to Satan for destruction of the flesh, so that the spirit might be saved in the day of the Lord.

Paul projects his own spirit into the Corinthians' worship: "when you have gathered and my spirit is with the power of our Lord Jesus." He is there with the risen Jesus, judging an egregious case of impurity.

Paul's presence in the spirit was no warm reassurance of his general good will but a searing judgment, spurning the nameless man, casting him out from the community into the world of the flesh, where destruction awaited him when God judged all people. Paul allowed for the possibility that such a person might finally be restored in spirit at the moment of apocalyptic destruction, but the fornicator had no part whatever in the transformed community of the faithful who enjoyed the presence and power of divine Spirit.

Paul plainly says that it is *he* who decides who belongs to the body of Christ and who does not, and that he does that at a distance, "in the spirit."

This is an example of Paul putting into practice the authority later called excommunication. The power to exclude people from the grace of forgiveness is also involved in Jesus' promise to Peter, whose name literally means "rock," in Matthew's Gospel (Matthew 16:18-19):

> And I say to you that you are Rock, and upon this rock I will build my congregation, and Hades' gates will not prevail over it. I will give you the keys of the kingdom of the heavens, and whatever you bind upon the earth shall have been bound in the heavens, and whatever you loose upon the earth shall have been loosed in the heavens.

The same promise is repeated in Matthew 18:18, where Jesus speaks to his disciples as a whole, showing that what he said to Peter treated Peter as a representative authority, not a unique agent of authority. In fact, the prior verse in Matthew speaks of regarding anyone who refuses the discipline of the Church as a whole "as a Gentile and a customs-agent" (Matthew 18:17).

Peter, like Paul, used the dark power of forgiveness, the decision to withhold it, in the service of Jesus' teaching. Jesus had advised a townsman to give away his property and follow with the other disciples (Mark 10:17-31, cf. Matthew 19:16-30 and Luke 18:18-30):

> He was proceeding out on a way and one ran up to him, and knelt to him, interrogated him, "Good teacher, what should I do so that I might inherit perpetual life?" But Jesus said to him, "Why do you say I am good? No one is good, except one: God! You know the decrees, Do not murder, do not commit adultery,

do not steal, do not witness falsely, do not deprive, honor your father and mother." But he told him, "Teacher, I have kept all these things from my youth." Yet Jesus looked at him, loved him, and said to him, "One thing is lacking you: depart, sell as much as you have and give to poor people, and you will have a store in heaven. And come on, follow me." But he was appalled at the word and went away grieving, because he had many effects. Jesus glared around and says to his students, "With what hardship will those who have possessions enter the kingdom of God!" But his students were astonished at his words; Jesus replied again and says to them, "Children, how hard it is to enter the kingdom of God! Easier for a camel to pass through a needle's hole than for a rich person to enter into the kingdom of God." But they were completely overwhelmed, saying to one another, "And who shall be saved?" Jesus looked at them, says: "Impossible with people, but not with God, because everything is possible with God." Rock began to say to him, "See: we left everything, and followed you." Jesus stated, "Amen I say to you, there is no one who has left home or brothers or sisters or mother or father or children or fields for my sake and the message's, except that shall receive a hundred times over—now in this time—homes and brothers and sisters and mothers and children and fields— with persecutions—and in the age that is coming perpetual life. But many first shall be last, and the last first."

According to the book of Acts, the apostolic community in Jerusalem that Peter headed put Jesus' advice into practice by their rule of communal possessions (Acts 4:34-35).

The ethos of that group is attested positively in the book of Acts by its praise of Barnabas, who was willing (as the anonymous townsman who met Jesus was not) to sell up property and follow with the other disciples (Acts 4:36-37). But there is also a negative—

and far more dramatic—attestation of this ethos, when Ananias and his wife Sapphira withhold a portion of the value of property they claim to have turned entirely over to the community. Interrogated by Peter, they are struck dead for lying against the Holy Spirit (Acts 5:1-11). Commentators will no doubt continue to debate whether Acts should be taken at face value in its description of the deaths of Ananias and Sapphira. However that issue is resolved, the fact remains that Acts endorses belief that God's power can harm as well as heal.

The story of Ananias and Sapphira exemplifies the dark power of withholding forgiveness. That power is exerted on the basis of the unbreakable connection between the ability to receive divine forgiveness and the ability to extend that forgiveness to others.[10] Because trust in God's capacity and will to forgive is part and parcel of receiving his grace, when trust is absent withholding forgiveness becomes the clearest endorsement of its value.

A policy of disposing of wealth in order to alleviate poverty is confirmed here and elsewhere in the traditions of the New Testament, along with a claim that those who rid themselves of financial wealth to adhere to an exchange economy will "receive a hundred times over—now in this time." Supported by the donations of others, and notably by contributions from Paul, the community in Jerusalem attempted to implement this policy more than any other church known to us during the ancient period. Peter and his companions, by means of their voluntary poverty for the sake of the movement, are assured of life everlasting. The passage reflects the stringent practice of Christianity in the circle of Jesus' followers that looked to Peter for leadership.

Peter's presentation of Jesus' teaching allowed for the possibility of rich people wriggling through the needle's eye. The analogy between Jesus' ministry and the voluntary acceptance of conditions typical of underclasses, however much it was recommended, was not taken by itself to be a fulfillment of the imperative to follow Jesus. That analogy was preferred, and even standard, and yet the analogy did not constitue an identity, such that simply accepting poverty made one like Jesus and worthy of eternal life. There was an awareness within Peter's circle, and within other communities of the New Testament, that the needle's eye was open for those with property, because voluntary poverty was at the service of a more basic means of enacting the ethos of the Christ, a principle that might be realized by programs other than voluntary poverty.

Jesus had said that the one sin that would not be forgiven was blasphemy against the Holy Spirit (Mark 3:29; Matthew 12:32; Luke 12:10), and in the case of Ananias and Sapphira, Peter took that to include an act of deceiving the community inhabited by that Spirit. Forgiveness, deriving from the compassion of God and answered with the compassion of faith, was an unbreakable foundation of a new relationship to God, as both Peter and Paul understood Jesus' teaching. But both those apostles also understood that the liberating force of forgiveness could and should be withheld from acts that denied Christ's Spirit, and that denial amounted to a lethal force.

This power, the dark side of forgiveness, needed to be directed against what harmed the community that gathered in Christ's Spirit, and the force, and even violence, of that power brings us to the next dimension of Jesus' teaching for transforming the world: the practice of mercy.

6
Mercy

Words sometimes exhibit a tendency to conceal more than they communicate.

Great founding figures of religious traditions—Mohandas Gandhi, Jesus, Martin Luther King, Jr., Krishna, Moses, Muhammad, Paul, and Peter, to take examples we have considered already—dedicated themselves to realities and visions that are not limited to this world. For that reason, they are often portrayed as not quite engaged with the world's needs. Sometimes they are even described as being "otherwordly" impatient of ordinary human vulnerability. Seeing beyond this world *seems* to imply a lack of care for it, according to a conventional use of language.

Is there, in fact, a shortage of compassion *caused* by the insight that this world and its suffering are transient and inconsequential? If a shortage of compassion shows up because suffering is seen as fleeting, that causal relation should show up clearly in the case of Buddhism. Among all the global religions, Buddhism is the most emphatic in its denial of the reality of the senses in favor of higher reality.

Yet according to authoritative tradition, the Buddha taught his followers the virtue that is usually called compassion, and he did so *as a matter of religious practice*:

Monks, you should carefully assume those practices which I have taught for the sake of direct knowledge. You should practice them, cultivate them, and make much of them, so that this religious practice will last for a long time, will be long standing. This is for the welfare of the multitudes, the happiness of the multitudes, the benefit, welfare, and happiness of gods and humans. This is out of sympathy with the world.[1]

In a careful examination of the language of the sources that has remained influential, Harvey B. Aronson[2] pointed out that the Buddha's concern for the world expressed much more engagement with others than the general public, and even some scholars, have associated with Buddhism.

Instead of a withdrawal from community and a refusal to become involved socially, which are attitudes commonly linked with Buddhism, the aim of the teaching of the Buddha (his *dharma*) was that all sentient beings should be happy, free of illness and trouble. The goal, in other words, was for liberation (*nirvana*) for others, and it was worth delaying one's own *nirvana* for the sake of others' advancement along that path.

This engagement on behalf of others' nirvana is proactive, and Aronson observes that the term for "compassion" (*karuna*) is not as frequently used as the term for "sympathy" (*anukampa*). That is an interesting observation, because it helps illustrate once again the limitations that words sometimes impose on analysis.

The English term "compassion" derives from the Latin roots for "suffering" (*passio*) and "with" (*con*), so that a compassionate person suffers along with a person in pain. The term "sympathy" derives from *exactly the same roots*, but in Greek (*pathe* for "suffering" and *sun* for with) rather than Latin. What Aronson is pointing to is that *usage*, rather than strict etymology, determines the meanings of words.

"Feeling for others" is the etymological meaning of *both* "compassion" and "sympathy," but in common speech "sympathy" seems to show more active concern, and implies more emotional engagement. Although these nuances swayed Aronson at the time he wrote, they are by no means fixed within English usage, and appear to be variable according to the period and location of dialects.

The difference that matters is not so much between words as it is between attitudes. The "loving mind" that wishes for the welfare of all sentient beings is what makes for the aim that Buddha teaches, whatever words one uses.

Just this imperative is conveyed in a memorable poem included in the canon of classic Buddhist recitations, which answers the question, "What should the person skilled in profitable practice do when he becomes aware of the peaceful state?"

One should cultivate an unlimited mind
Toward all beings
The way a mother protects her only son
With her life.

He should cultivate an unlimited loving mind,
    without obstruction, anger, or opposition
To the whole world
Above, below, and across.

Standing, walking, sitting, or reclining,
He should be resolute in this mindfulness,
As long as he is free from fatigue.
Here this is called the sublime attitude.[3]

How can an attitude possibly include motherly care *and* sublime indifference? Texts of Buddhism explore this paradox better than any other resources, but the paradox itself is rooted in the prophetic perspective as a whole.

Jesus made his way to a realization of this attitude more through experience than through conscious meditation. One lesson of Jesus' life came to him when he made his way back to Nazareth after his time with John the Baptist, a much longer period than a superficial reading of the Gospels would suggest.[4] Because the adolescent Jesus had spent a considerable period with John while convention dictated he should remain at home, his return to his native village was emotionally fraught.

The little agricultural hamlet of Nazareth was set on the side of a rocky hill, protected by a string of mountains north of the Valley of Jezreel. Jesus came up the hill from the south, savoring the familiar configuration of the pastures, fields, and groves. The Galileans harvested barley during the spring. Men cut the crop with powerful thrusts of their iron-bladed shoulder scythes. Women and children gathered the whiskery stalks into sheaves and dragged them across the fields to their courtyards, where they set them out to dry on grass mats under the eaves of their homes.

There is no report of exactly what happened when Jesus, unheralded and unexpected, walked into town on that early summer day in 21 C.E. But after he had become a master of parables, he embedded his homecoming experience in his parable of the prodigal son. In this vivid and hyperbolic story (Luke 15:11-32), a wayward son is reduced to pig-tending for a Gentile after leaving home and squandering the inheritance he had precipitately asked his father to give him as he left town.

When the son at last is forced by his poverty and hunger to return home in abject humiliation, his father treats him like a prince, ordering a fattened calf to be slaughtered for a celebratory feast. An older brother, trudging back from the field, is angry and jealous when a servant explains what is happening. The father is sympathetic with the elder son, but firm in regard to his attitude (Luke 15:32): "It was necessary to celebrate and rejoice, because your brother was dead and lives, was lost and is found."

There was no fatted calf for Jesus. Probably none was available in the poor village of Nazareth, and in any case the meal is prepared much more quickly in the parable than would have been possible in reality. By this time, in any event, the Gospels intimate that Joseph had died, so that Miriam (the Semitic form of the name translated as Mary) became the effective head of her household.

But Miriam greeted Jesus as eagerly as the prodigal's doting father. James, named first among Jesus' brothers in Mark 6:3, is clearly the older brother in the parable of the prodigal son. James would naturally have resented Jesus' joyous welcome by Miriam after the disgrace Jesus had brought on the family by abandoning them to become a disciple of John the Baptist. But for Jesus this return to Nazareth ended a long and dangerous nomadic period, and the emotional healing of his mother's embrace resonates in his parable of the prodigal come home.

The conviction that God's care is like a parent's, only greater than any human mother's or father's, is rooted deeply in the Scriptures of Israel. The book of Isaiah includes striking reassurances that God's compassion extends beyond even the deepest human forms of compassion:

Can a woman forget her nursing baby, not to have mercy on the son of her belly? Even they might forget, but I will not forget. (Isaiah 49:15)

For you are our father, although Abraham does not know us and Israel does not acknowledge us. You, LORD, are our father, our deliverer; your name is eternal. (Isaiah 63:16)

These clear statements contradict two widely accepted fallacies.

First, the Scriptures of Israel are quite emphatic, as Jesus was, that God's care was like a parent's. The frequently heard claim that "the God of the Old Testament" was austere, while Jesus originated the address of God as father, is simply untrue.

Second, the two assertions in Isaiah show that God's love could be and was compared with that of *any* parent, male or female. The idea that the God of Israel was uniquely patriarchal, and that Jesus perpetuated the conception in male-only symbolism for God, is a modern distortion.

In fact, of course, the book of Isaiah introduces the imagery of the mother before that of the father, and that priority makes sense from the point of view of how divine care is described. The verb for "having mercy" (*racham*) in Hebrew appears as a noun in order to mean "womb." The term reflects that deep, visceral connection between mother and child, which a father, at least a good father, can also feel.

The Aramaic tradition that survives from Jesus' time expresses a powerful principle in its translation of Leviticus 22:28 (in the Targum Pseudo-Jonathan), "My people, children of Israel, since I am merciful in heaven, so should you be merciful upon the earth." The expansion in the Targum is unquestionably innovative, because the Hebrew text speaks simply of not killing an animal and her young on the same day.

From that injunction, the Aramaic interpreters articulated a universal requirement of mercy, which is echoed by Jesus in Luke 6:36, within the address known conventionally as "the sermon on the plain" (the equivalent in Luke of Matthew's "sermon on the mount"):

Become merciful, just as your Father is also merciful.

In biblical terms, "mercy" is the best way to describe how God's active care and concern should be taken up by his children, and it is interesting that the word *anukampa* in Buddhism is also often rendered as "mercy." Whatever term is used, in whatever tradition, the grounding wisdom of the prophetic perspective urges people to love with the intimacy of a parent and yet with the assurance that the storms of temporal life can be managed from within the still, strong eye of eternity.

Jesus used that wisdom to address what he considered the most terrible burden of his time. In the last chapter, we saw that within the Gospels, a coherent language of "debt" is attributed to Jesus. When, in the Matthean version of the Lord's Prayer, Jesus instructs his followers to ask God, "forgive us our debts, as we also forgive our debtors," there is no doubt but that the New Testament is preserving an Aramaic idiom (6:12). Luke preserves the usage only partially: "Forgive us our sins, as we also forgive everyone who is indebted to us" (11:4). Sometimes the reader who searches for Jesus' original expressions is put in the position of an archaeologist, who has to sift through layers of later material in order to find evidence for the period under investigation beneath these later accretions.

Jesus' recourse to the Aramaic idiom of debt as sin is not only a matter of standard convention. Several of his parables turn on the metaphorical and literal senses of "debt," and extend the comparison. In particular, Jesus' use of the term reflects a usage also found in the Aramaic Targum of Isaiah.

In the Targum of Isaiah, the term "debt" refers in one breath to money literally owed, and in another breath to sins before God (Isaiah Targum 50:1, italics added, to indicate innovations in the Aramaic text in comparison to the Hebrew text):

> Thus says the LORD, "Where is *the* bill of divorce which I *gave* your *congregation, that it is rejected*? Or who *had a debt against me*, to whom I have sold you? Behold, for your *debts* you were sold, and for your *apostasies* your *congregation* was *rejected.*"

The first usage of "debt" corresponds well to the underlying idea in the Hebrew text of Isaiah, which refers to creditors. The second usage of "debt" represents "iniquities" in the Hebrew text.

The same word does duty for two different Hebrew terms. In both cases, the choice of diction represents a good technique of translation. Yet both translations together produce a uniquely Targumic connection of "debt" in its literal and metaphorical senses, as in the usage of Jesus.

In several of his most memorable parables Jesus extended the meaning of "debt" in a way consonant with the Targum's contrast between the debilitating condition of owing money and the power of God's forgiveness. This extension of meaning represents Jesus' conviction that forgiveness is not only a possibility but also that God in his mercy *demands* that his children extend forgiveness to others.

In Matthew 18:23-35, a debtor is said to owe the astronomical sum of ten thousand talents (18:24). When it is borne in mind that the annual imposition of tax by Herod Antipas upon the whole of

Galilee and Peraea amounted to merely two hundred talents (see Josephus, *Antiquities* 17.11.4 §319), the hyperbole involved in the parable becomes readily apparent. A single talent amounts to some seventy-five pounds of precious metal, unimaginable wealth for all but the most powerful people of Jesus' time.

The debtor in this parable is in absolutely no position to repay his debt. There is not even any credible way in which he could have incurred the debt. Yet after his debt is forgiven (v. 27), the debtor behaves in a way that is as stupid as his debt was large. His conduct seems calculated to trivialize the enormous forgiveness he was received, when he refuses (vv. 28-30) to deal mercifully with a colleague who owed him one hundred denarii.

One hundred denarii amounted to a considerable sum: a single denarius has been estimated as the going rate for a full day of labor.[5] But the contrast with the king's incalculable generosity cannot be overlooked, and the close of the parable makes it unmistakably plain that God's forgiveness demands ours (vv. 31-35). To fail to forgive one's fellow, even when what needs to be forgiven is considerable, is to betray the very logic of forgiveness that alone gives us standing before God. Mercy in Jesus' teaching is more than advice: it becomes a demand, sanctioned by God's judgment.

Two other parables that we considered in the last chapter also portray, in an apparently paradoxical fashion, the inextricable link between divine forgiveness and human behavior. Within the story of Jesus at the house of a Pharisee named Simon (Luke 7:36-50), a parable explains why Jesus chose to forgive a sinful woman (vv. 40-43). Of two debtors, the one who has been released from the greater debt will obviously love his creditor more. The sinful woman's great love, therefore, in an outlandish display of affection and honor (vv. 37-38, 44-46), is proof that God had forgiven her

(v. 47). Her love demonstrates her capacity to be forgiven.[6] She had succeeded precisely where the unforgiving servant of Matthew 18 had failed: her actions displayed the value of forgiveness to her. The same logic, developed more strictly in respect of debt, is evident in the otherwise inexplicable parable of the crafty steward (Luke 16:1-9), whose deliberate surrealism we explored in the last chapter.

The metaphorical usage of "debt" attributed to Jesus in the Gospels, therefore, is initially to be understood as an Aramaism. He exploited the metaphorical possibilities of the term in a way that is precedented in the Targum of Isaiah, but in his own characteristically parabolic fashion. The general activity of telling parables, it has been established, is well attested among early rabbis.[7] At issue here is not Jesus' absolute uniqueness, but the relative distinctiveness that distinguishes any significantly historical figure from his contemporaries.

A well-established metaphor of early Judaism spoke not only of debts but also of credit in respect of God.[8] Jesus extended that metaphor, as well (cf. Matthew 6:19-21; 19:21-22; Mark 10:21; Luke 12:33, 34; 18:22). But it was in his adaptation of the idiom and theology of "debt" in his parables that Jesus developed a characteristic aspect of his message as a whole.

Metaphorical insight, along with the insistence that God's mercy demands human generosity in response, pervades another famous parable of Jesus, the parable of the talents (Matthew 25:14-30). Talents are things that people today expect just about everyone has, especially in America. Mark Twain once remarked that our myth about having talent gets in the way of our willingness to work hard enough to become good at what we do.

How we usually think of "talent" can be both helpful and obstructive in understanding Jesus' parable in Matthew 25:14-30. Helpful, because common English is actually influenced by the parable: we do not primarily think of a talent as a unit of payment at all but rather as a gift that God endows us with. But also obstructive, because there is a tendency to imagine that God's gift is simply there naturally, a routine inheritance that comes so easily it can be used or not with little or no cost.

Jesus consciously chose the metaphor of the talent, as the largest unit of currency he could conceive of, seventy pounds or more of gold, silver, or copper. As we have seen, that was not something most people Jesus spoke to had ever encountered in their lives. Jesus deliberately referred to talents in order to convey the idea of unimaginable wealth. The parable of the unforgiving debtor in Matthew 18:23-35 speaks of owing a myriad talents. Jesus was speaking there, almost as a child would, of an astronomical sum.

Why did Jesus use these outlandish numbers? He did so because he was referring to an overwhelming reality, whether the debt we owe to God (in the parable of the unforgiving debtor) or the riches God bestows on us (in the parable of the talents). In the Aramaic language, "debt" was the usual way to refer to sin, and Jesus extended that usage consciously in the parable of the unforgiving debtor. Then, in the parable of the talents, he pushes the image further still: we owe God, not only the deficit we have incurred, but an account for the wealth he has given us in trust.

Jesus' deliberate hyperbole, his surrealism about money, is more easily understood when his own economic background is remembered. The economy of the small villages and hamlets that Jesus frequented did not function day to day on the basis of currency. Currency indeed featured prominently when regions paid their tax to Rome, and in the great cities that grew up within Roman hegemony in Galilee and Judea. But what is stunning about Jesus' travels is that he did not frequent the great cities that recent archaeological work has taught us much about: Tiberias, Sepphoris, or Caesarea. He avoided those places in favor of Capernaum about as easily as he dismissed Caesar's coin (see Matthew 22:21; Mark 12:17; Luke 20:25) as of small importance compared to what is God's.

In the rural Galilee that was the primary focus of Jesus' movement, currency was not the ordinary medium of commerce. That kind of moneyed transaction, which grew up in urban environments and now dominates our daily practice and thinking, was simply not the rule. Indeed, not even barter was the norm. A person from one village might barter with a person from another village, and trade with currency might happen with a city, but within the village the exchange of goods and services would occur on the basis of people's status in that place.

By the reasoning of a traditional society, the status of belonging to a community entitles people, with their various abilities and weaknesses, to the living that community can provide. That is one reason Jesus focused on small rural communities: in a village, the policy of giving freely and taking freely was already established (see Matthew 10:8). Part of Jesus' purpose was, in the name of God's Kingdom, to supplant the economy based on currency with an economy based on exchange. Instead of making the city the model of Israel, the village was to show the way to all God's people.

That is why, when Jesus does speak of currency, the imagery is surreal. He is not talking about actual financial amounts in the experience of the people he is speaking to, nor is he advocating any action they could be expected to imitate literally. Rather, the currency is symbolic of the unimaginable wealth involved when we owe God, whether for our sin or in return for his favor.

Jesus' symbolism is so obvious that most people grasp intuitively that wealth was not on his mind when he spoke of debts or talents. Several years ago I attended a useful series of conferences in Europe, modeled on the prayer breakfasts in Washington. At one of them, which took place at Windsor Castle, a speaker explained the parable of the talents: God appeared as a master capitalist, and he expected a return on his investments. The unease in the room during this address was palpable, and many of those who attended commented on their discomfort later, when we met socially.

The audience would not have been invited to Windsor unless they enjoyed some wealth and success, and yet they simply did not feel right about being told that wealth and success was what God wanted from them.

People of wealth—a designation that includes most people living in the United States today—understand that they do not need encouragement to make yet more money. Their problem, on the contrary, is the narrowness of the eye of the needle and how to get through it (see Matthew 19:23-26; Mark 10:23-27; Luke 18:24-27). When Jesus speaks of "talents," he does not refer primarily to monetary investment; his target is the divine endowment that has been bestowed on us all. And the worst thing, the one and only bad thing, that can be done with that trust is not to expand on it. Just keeping it safe and hidden is precisely what Jesus does not want; in this regard again, the investment he speaks of is strange because risks are not to be avoided. Stagnation is worse than risk because the aim of what we do with God's talents should be their extension.

Those of us at the conference at Windsor did not need to be comforted in our wealth; we needed to be challenged over what we do with our talents. We, and most people I come in contact with, have to find places where we can exchange and extend God's precious talents, despite the pressures of the economy of Caesar's money that almost all of us live in and with.

Religious congregations are just such places. Beyond their pledges and investments and properties, they are communities of talent, villages of hope where we may take freely and give freely in the name of the Kingdom. Because we gather in our congregations, not as individuals but as people of God, we can there exchange the wealth of God's grace, and in that exchange can discover what it is to enter into the joy of our master.

The awareness of being sheltered as a community by God's mercy, and living under the demand of mercy, also makes Jesus' demand to love enemies not only the behavior prompted by the gift of insight (as we saw in chapter 4) but a requirement of social living. The First Letter of Peter spells out this policy for its community (1 Peter 4:14-19) during a time of severe persecution near the end of the first century:

> If you are reviled for the name of Christ, you are blessed, because the Spirit of glory—even God's own Spirit—rests upon you. Because none of you is to suffer as a murderer or thief or doer of bad or meddler: but if as a Christian, let him not be ashamed, but give glory to God by this name. Because now is time for judgment to begin with the house of God; and if first with us, what will the end be of those who disobey the gospel of God? And if the just person is barely saved, where shall the irreverent and the sinful appear? So let those who suffer according to the will of God commend their lives to a faithful creator in doing good.

The reality of suffering at the hands of opponents is not only acknowledged but celebrated, because the pain of the present time, a function of the injustice of this world, is transitional to the glory that is to come. The only real danger is that Christians might begin to commit injustice since they are treated as criminals in any case. The letter addresses just that worry, while it firmly articulates a classic response to the reality of unjustly suffering pain.

Right through the New Testament, from Jesus to the First Letter of Peter, living by the rule of God's mercy includes an ethic of exemplary response. This teaching is not only for individuals but also for communities. This is worth stressing because in the history of Christian thought, theologians have tried to wriggle away from this imperative by claiming that, in the affairs of nations, exemplary response is not a practical policy.

State-sanctioned violence is often justified by thinly disguised arguments for vengeance, and even—as in the case of the recent American invasion of Iraq—on the theory that preemptive violence is justifiable. Events there have taught us again what both the Ten Commandments and Jesus warned us of: when you have recourse to institutions of violence, you should not be surprised if you have to pay the last penny (see Matthew 5:25-26), and payment might be required in the coin of your own children (Exodus 20:5). In the affairs of nations, as in the lives of individuals, preemptive grace is the only policy with a future because it realizes divine mercy. Apologists for violence are false prophets.

At the same time, God's mercy cannot depend on the institutions of this world. Jesus was no more sanguine about Roman courts than he was about Roman soldiers. That is why he gave his advice in regard to reconciling with enemies (Matthew 5:25-26):

> Be well disposed with your opponent quickly, while you are with
> him on the way; otherwise, the opponent will deliver you over to
> the judge, and the judge to the assistant, and you will be thrown
> into prison. Amen I say to you, you will not get out of there until
> you have paid the last quadrans.

Those who believe this advice is impractical miss Jesus' prophetic suspicion of human institutions, a suspicion which the results of unnecessary litigation show was realistic.

More important, they miss Jesus' radical re-vision of how we are to work out our love of God. Every person is made in God's own image and likeness, and mirrors some of the truth of the divine presence, because God creates everyone that way (Genesis 1:26-27). Jesus, like Buddha, saw that we are all intimately connected—what we do to others we do to ourselves, in actions rich with future consequences.

The prophetic challenge of human institutions includes criticizing the ingrained nationalism of many people in the world. Americans, for example, have put "In God we trust" on their money for so long that they sometimes behave as if that arrangement were reciprocal. The blessings we enjoy are indeed incalculable, whether reckoned in comparison to the fortunes of most people in the world today or on the basis of what human experience until our time has taught us. But endowment with blessing is no proof of merit, although it is only human to believe that we have earned what we have (and that our hardships are undeserved). We are understandably proud of our form of democracy, and we often see it as the engine of our prosperity. So when it seems to fall apart, we become deeply concerned.

From a biblical point of view, it is in any case strange to think of government as trustworthy. "Put not your trust in princes" (Psalm

146:3) is a typical admonition, because the brokenness that is a part of our identity as human beings does not simply disappear when we organize into nations. Part of the genius of our own political system, in fact, is that it recognizes the sin embedded in human nature and seeks to contain it by checks, balances, and a willingness to change, instead of pretending that sin can be removed or ignored.

When Jesus laconically said, "Caesar's repay to Caesar, and God's to God" (Mark 12:17), he certainly did not assume that Caesar was just. His experience taught him that the opposite was true. With other Galileans, he hoped that God's Kingdom would supplant Caesar's kingdom, and every human hegemony. Government for Jesus was not a blessing or even an instrument of justice (as it could be in St. Paul's mind) but a simple fact of life, which you accepted as part of what God desired to transform.

If the rulers of this world, even the democratically selected ones, do not seem to come anywhere near to the measure of God's Kingdom, that is no surprise. What is surprising is that we are disappointed when their human nature shows up in their actions in the form of self-interested ploys. The fault line between what people actually try to gain when they have power and the aspirations they strive for is a perennial breach in the constitution of humanity.

The last book of the New Testament, the Revelation of John, provoked controversy within the ancient Church, and has done so until our day. More than any other writing in early Christianity, the Revelation speaks from the point of view that God has a plan to overthrow and replace all the powerful institutions of this world. The seer who writes from the island of Patmos with the common name "John" (*Yochanan* in Aramaic) speaks with a voice unlike that of the Gospel of John or the Johannine Epistles, invoking a scenario of violence and retribution alongside complex visions of the Throne of God. Through it all, however, the author attempts to envisage how God's judgment and God's mercy go hand in hand, and how both go beyond what any human institution or convention can imagine.

Fitting the Revelation into the great themes of the New Testament—such as Paul's teaching of justification by grace and Jesus' insistence on the overriding imperative to love, to embrace even our enemies—is at least as difficult as coming to grips with the difficult issues of who exactly wrote this document, and why. The whole book is (in a word) so apocalyptic that it can seem hard to square with the pattern of Christian faith, ancient or modern.

The Greek name of this visionary manifesto, *apocalypsis,* actually gave us the word "apocalyptic" in English. Yet however strange it may seem, the Revelation of John focuses on exactly the kind of visions attributed to Jesus in the Gospels, for example at his baptism and during his temptations in the wilderness, although the Gospels report visions only episodically, and not in great depth. Even Paul speaks of being snatched up into the third heaven (2 Corinthians 12:3, 4). He says he cannot articulate what he was told in his ecstasy: in the case of the Revelation, the depth and intensity of the visionary experience is brought to full expression, and that naturally makes us pause.

Living as we now do in times that are frightening and unstable, where innocents suffer unpredictably at the hands of irrationally hateful forces, perhaps we now have ears to hear the Revelation. Churches at ease, basically comfortable with the world as it is, have found the Revelation's apocalyptic idiom extreme and obscure. But the modern culture of conflict has brought us individually and collectively to an awareness of the impermanence and violence of our lives.

The key of the Revelation is not doctrine as much as it is emotion, the visceral anxiety of communities under pressure from their Roman masters. The signature lament of the book is the simple, striking question, "How long?" Beneath the heavenly altar, the visionary reality that remained after the destruction of the physical Temple by the Romans in 70 C.E., the seer sees and recognizes "the souls slain for the word of God and for the witness they maintained" (Revelation 6:9-10). It is they who ask, "How long, holy and true master, do you not judge and vindicate our blood from those who dwell upon the earth?"

Those who have suffered lament not only the loss of their lives but the injustice that persists in the world. D. H. Lawrence excoriated this plea for revenge as a distortion of Jesus' message.[9] But the situation is very much as in the Psalms, where the poet often speaks from the point of view of innocent suffering. We might desire not to be vengeful when we are injured, but that should not prevent us from seeing that Scripture articulates a deeply human response to injustice, a sense of rage and pain at one and the same time.

Denying the rage and the pain does not make it disappear. The Revelation, like the Psalms, develops a response to the human sense of injury and grievance. The Revelation addresses the suffering condition of the faithful by means of its visions of God, especially of the Throne of God. The divine Throne, the place of both judgment and healing within Jesus' teaching and much of the Judaism of his time, is the constant focus of the seer of Patmos.

John's vision of the Throne of God, as set out in chapters 4 and 5, is the pivot of his book as a whole. He sees the divine source of creation in the way Moses and Ezekiel did, combining the language of Exodus 24 and Ezekiel 1 with Zechariah's insight into the Spirit that emanates from the divine presence (Zechariah 4). Steeped as this vision is in the biblical apocalypse of the divine Throne, it also incorporates the distinctively Christian experience of Jesus' resurrection. Jesus appears *on* God's Throne, the lamb that was slain (Revelation 5:6). His slaying was also his exaltation, what joined him to the Throne of God.

The lamb's triumph elicits a hymn of praise (Revelation 5:9-10):

> For you were slain and have redeemed us to God by your blood out of every clan and tongue and people and nation. And you have made us a kingdom and priests to God, and they shall reign upon earth.

The one who was slain vindicates all the suffering of innocents because his death exalted him to the very center of divine mercy.

John of the Revelation knew no stability in his world, yet by means of vision he identified the presence of God as the unique, stable reality. His language is ornate, but that only underscores how creative primitive Christian prophecy was in its adaptation of biblical apocalypse and its faith in the risen Jesus.

Those of us who have sensed only recently that our world is passing away, that what seemed stable is fragile, that what claims to be just can be destructive, can learn from the Revelation. Precisely because it includes the dark, retributive side of human anxiety, it teaches that the vision of God, focused by means of those Scriptural images that convey most to us of divine reality, will prove to be our anchor in a wild sea of change.

Living in the midst of uncertainty, relying entirely upon the mercy of God and upon those who have learned to be merciful, involves coming to terms with one's own rage, but also with one's vulnerability. That happened to Paul during the time of his final imprisonment. For the first time in his life, he relied directly on other people for his daily needs. Custody for a citizen did not involve punitive imprisonment, but paying for his housing, food, serving staff, guardians, and occasional bribes to officials quickly depleted Paul's funds. Prohibited from pursuing his craft of making and repairing tents, he ate up what remained of the collection he had taken among churches for an "offering of the Gentiles" (Romans 15:16); he had hoped to bring that into the Jerusalem Temple as the crown of his ministry, a sacrifice in which both Jews and Gentiles would have participated. But he had been arrested by the Romans in Jerusalem, and now he had to render Caesar his due from funds he had collected for his offering. After those funds were gone, he had to turn to his friends.

Paul needed deep relationships to sustain him. Timothy became his closest friend. He was now much more than just a young assistant willing to do anything—even be circumcised—to help Paul prove a point. He increasingly spoke for Paul, and composed letters with him in which he also expressed his own concerns.

Paul's letters become sporadic at this point, and he speaks in a new idiom. There are no longer triumphant appeals to the power of Christian mission to hasten the end of the world, or references to Paul's overwhelming spiritual authority as an apostle. At the close of his triumphant progress to the Temple he had found only ashes, and the result is that in the little he did write, we see Paul's own broken mortality, and, at the same time, his affective connection to other people.

In 58 C.E., he and Timothy wrote a private letter to a wealthy slaveholder they had met back in Ephesus named Philemon.[10]

Paul's whole concern in these twenty-five short verses is with a slave Philemon had loaned him, named Onesimus. Onesimus had stayed on in Caesarea with Paul longer than originally agreed, and Paul wanted to spare the man punishment from an irate Philemon (vv. 8-10): "So having much confidence in Christ to order you what is proper, for love's sake I rather appeal—being Paul the senior, but now also a prisoner for Jesus Christ—I appeal to you concerning my child, whom I begat in my bonds, Onesimus."

Paul's new tenderness brought no new modesty, false or otherwise, as the opening of this statement shows. But the whole focus is his deep attachment to Onesimus, a feeling he experiences, he says, deep in his body: his viscera (*splangkhna* in Greek). Sadly, modern commentators have tended to weaken the meaning of this term to "heart," but the King James Version bravely uses "bowels." The sense of the term, however, comes from *racham* in Semitic languages, the visceral mercy of God. Cut off by the forced repose of custody from his usual, high-voltage activity, Paul became aware of his visceral link (vv. 7, 20) with people as close to him as the children he never had.

Despite the hectic anxiety of his custody and appeal, and the politics Paul played to stay out of reach of the high priest and get himself to Rome, the bustle of travel over land and sea, he wrote to the Philippians in his calmest, most limpid piece of writing. He longs for the Philippians, he said, "in the viscera of Jesus Christ" (Philippians 1:8; see 2:1). Yes, he needed money, but not much, and he acknowledged (Philippians 4:18) his European children had already sent him enough money to see him to Rome.

Timothy—his "son" as Paul calls him (Philippians 2:19-22)—is the designated emissary for further contact once he has arrived in Rome, but Epaphroditus—whom Paul calls "your apostle" (2:25)—

is on his way back from Myra to Philippi after an illness (2:25-30). He had already delivered a gift that seemed lavish to Paul (4:18): "a fragrant aroma, a sacrifice acceptable, pleasing to God." The connection Paul once sought to forge by collecting funds on behalf of others is now consummated with the concern of others for him.

Paul's affection suffuses this letter, as well as his deliberate emphasis on how to concentrate his thoughts (*phronein*) on people in Philippi while he is in custody (Philippians 1:3-7). This thinking of himself and of them, the deliberate orientation of one's own mind and heart in difficulty, is his focus throughout the letter, as he refers circumstantially to the military personnel (1:13) that escorted him.

Paul's mood became so valedictory, he could even refer to his old competitors with something like affection, although he did not give an inch when it came to his principles or his pride (1:15-18): "Some herald Christ from jealousy and contention, and some from a good desire. Those who act from love know that I am destined for a defense of the gospel; those who act from ambition proclaim Christ, not purely, supposing they raise tribulation by my bonds. So what? As long as in every way, whether by pretext or truth, Christ is proclaimed—and in this I rejoice!"

This is no "born again" Paul: he calls people who want to circumcise Gentile believers "dogs," "evil-doers," "the mutilation" (Philippians 3:2). He made his way to Rome with a new maturity, a fresh reticence, but his adolescent joy in rhetoric never failed him. What did await him in Rome? Should he hope for life or death? Paul doesn't know (Philippians 1:20-22). He lived in a truncated present where all his expectations had been disappointed, and yet new lineaments of affection grow and prosper. To be free of life's concerns entirely and serve Christ in Spirit is his desire, and yet he remembers people like the Philippians themselves (1:23-24): "I am constrained between the two—having the greater and better desire to cast off and be with Christ *and* as more necessary for you to persevere in the flesh." He entered a netherworld, living on the cusp of life and death, willing for either, accepting both, in a way that the Buddha's teaching advises.

After years of saying that various readers should imitate him, just as he imitates Christ—a touching imperative if you liked Paul, obvious arrogance if you did not—with little preamble he tells the Philippians what that whole process is about (2:5-8): "Let this mind be in you, which was also in Christ Jesus; who, being in the form of God, thought it not robbery to be equal with God: But made himself of no reputation, and took upon him the form of a servant, and was made in the likeness of men: And being found in fashion as a man, he humbled himself, and became obedient unto death, even the death of the cross."

This language is so resonant, it has been described as a hymn—and attributed to a liturgical song that Paul quotes.[11] But even if that is so, Paul is the author who uses this language to speak deliberately of Jesus as God. He has broken through to poetry and enlists the Philippians in working out the deeply affective salvation that was to be their inheritance (2:12-13) by embracing the mind of Christ. The simplicity of the whole achievement is staggering. Paul can now write what is commonly used as a blessing at the close of many, many liturgies, "The peace of God that passes all understanding will keep your hearts and thoughts in Jesus Christ" (4:7). Jesus now becomes the focus of faith, because he is divine and is revealed within the believer so that God's thoughts become human thoughts. "At the name of Jesus every knee shall bow, in heaven, on earth, and in the underworld" (2:10): Christ receives the honor due God because he makes humanity divine.[12]

Paul is too detached to become as emotionally charged as he once did. "To write the same things to you is not troublesome to me, but is necessary for you" (3:1). These are not the words of someone burning to write. The force of argument in his prose had been replaced by lyricism. Paul's analysis of the mystical union between Christ and believers was making him into a different kind of writer, a poet, in spite of himself, of the mercy of God.

7
Glory

"Glory" is the consistent translation of terms used in the Scriptures of Israel—Hebrew *kavod*, Aramaic *yaqara'*, and Greek *doxa*—to refer to the medium in which God himself exists. The substance of the divine is obviously not of our world, yet in the biblical conception it constitutes the enduring reality that lies behind our world. "Glory" denotes weight or substance and at the same time connotes light and radiance. Glory is alien from the point of view of the medium in which people live day to day. In the Bible people ordinarily cannot even see God but instead are dazzled by the impenetrable brilliance of his Glory.

A classic scene of God's exceptional appearance to a human being in the substance of his Glory occurs when Moses receives instructions from Yahweh (Exodus 24:15-18):

> Moses went up the mountain, and the cloud covered the mountain. Yahweh's Glory dwelled upon Mount Sinai, and the cloud covered it six days, and he called to Moses the seventh day from the midst of the cloud. The appearance of the Glory of Yahweh was like a consuming fire on top of the mountain to the eyes of the sons of Israel. Moses went into the midst of the cloud and

went up the mountain. Moses was on the mountain forty days
and forty nights.

For most people, at most times, and in most places, Glory is so
unlike the stuff of their world that they cannot even look into it,
much less enter into God's Glory. Moses is here portrayed as an
exception.

The ancient Israelite conception of God's substance was not that
Glory was ethereal or insubstantial in comparison to the experience of this world. The reverse was the case: God was a weightier
and stronger presence than human perception could usually conceive or endure. It required a special disclosure for any person to
be able to see through the passing, comparatively insubstantial
reality of human society into the enduring, dynamic reality of God.
Moses was one such extraordinary person.

The vision of Jesus' Transfiguration, we have already seen in
chapter 3, showed Jesus sharing divine glory with Moses and
Elijah, and conveying the power of his association with the greatest prophets of Israel to three of his disciples. Part of the attractive—and at the same time disruptive—influence of Jesus'
perspective on those around him was his conviction that God's
Glory, a substance literally weightier and more powerful than any
physical reality, was coming into the world and transforming it.
The disciples made this conviction their own after Jesus' death.
Their belief in Jesus' resurrection, and their hope that they would
enjoy eternal life after death, was grounded in the confidence that
human beings had been made by God to share in divine Glory.

Paul, whose conception of the resurrection we will investigate in
greater detail only after a discussion of Jesus' own conception of
the glorious existence that is possible for people, shows clearly that
early Christians saw Glory as the medium of who *they* were to be,

together with God. Paul crafted a metaphysical language of resurrection to refer to a reality beyond this world that nonetheless unmakes and remakes this world (1 Corinthians 15:35-44, written ca. 55 C.E.):

> But someone will say, "How are the dead raised, and with what sort of body do they come?" Fool, what you yourself sow does not become alive unless it dies! And what you sow—it is not the body that shall be that you sow—is but a bare germ, perhaps of wheat or of another grain. But God gives to it a body just as he wills, and to each of the seeds its own body. Not all flesh is the same flesh, but one of humans, another flesh of animals, another flesh of birds, another of fish. And there are heavenly bodies and earthly bodies, but one is the glory of the heavenly and another of the earthly. Sun's glory is one and moon's glory another, and another stars' glory, because star differs from star in glory. So also is the resurrection of the dead. Sown in decay, it is raised in incorruption; sown in dishonor, it is raised in Glory; sown in weakness, it is raised in power; sown a physical body, it is raised a spiritual body.

In the whole of Christian literature, there is not a more exact statement of the process of resurrection, and Paul's words have had a firm place in Christian liturgies of burial. Their particular genius is the insight that resurrection involves a new creative act by God, what Paul elsewhere calls a "new creation" (2 Corinthians 5:17; Galatians 6:15). Morally and existentially, the hope of the resurrection involves a fresh, fulfilled humanity: "sown in dishonor, it is raised in Glory."

In literary terms, 1 Corinthians is Paul's greatest achievement, and perhaps the finest single piece of writing in the New Testament. It is rich in insight, theology, and emotion, beautifully coordinated to the specific circumstances addressed, and filled with prose so vivid—especially as rendered in the King James Version—it can take its stand alongside the poetry of any culture.

The full significance of Paul's teaching, however, cannot be appreciated without a working knowledge of what Jesus taught. Jesus pictured life with God as involving such a radical change that ordinary human relationships would no longer prevail. That conviction of a radical change brought with it a commitment to the language of eschatology, of the ultimate transformation that God both promised and threatened.

Efforts have often been made in modern interpretation to discount the eschatological dimension of Jesus' teaching. They have not prevailed. Periodically, theologians in the West have attempted to convert Jesus' perspective into their own sense that the world is a stable and changeless entity, but that appears to have been far from his own orientation.[1] Jesus' commitment to eschatology is a matter of common agreement in scholarly evaluations of his view of the Kingdom of God.

But what of Jesus' understanding of what is to happen, not with the world at large but *to particular human beings* within God's disclosure of his Kingdom? Resurrection, in the faith and teaching of virtually all churches for nearly two millennia, promises actual life to individual persons within God's global transformation of all things. Because Jesus, on a straightforward reading of the Gospels, does not say much about resurrection as such, there has been a lively dispute over whether he had any distinctive, or even specific, teaching in that regard.

Still, in the single case when Jesus does address this issue, his contribution proves to be unequivocal and lucid. Sadducees are portrayed in the Synoptic Gospels as asking a mocking question of

Jesus, designed to disprove the possibility of resurrection (see Mark 12:18-23; cf. Matthew 22:23-28; Luke 20:27-33). Their question sets up a hypothesis in order to ridicule Jesus' teaching, and Jesus replies to them.

The Sadducees' exact motives for entering into this dispute, apart from their increasing antipathy to Jesus in the period involving his intervention in the Temple, are a matter of conjecture. Acts 23:8 makes out that the Sadducees denied resurrection altogether, and that is also the judgment of Josephus. But I have argued that, despite these unequivocal statements—or rather, precisely because they feature among very broad accusations that the Sadducees' opponents allege against them—we should be cautious about what the Sadducees denied.[2] It seems more likely to me that they denied that resurrection is a direct teaching of the Torah, and held it might be a possible belief, without being in any sense a mandatory doctrine.

Whatever the full extent of their motivations, the Sadducees in Mark's Gospel, which presents the earliest version of the argument, set out their hypothetical case: because Moses commanded that, were a man to die childless, his brother should raise up a seed for him (Deuteronomy 25:5-6); suppose there were seven brothers, the first of whom was married. If all the brothers died childless in sequence, whose wife would the woman be in the resurrection?

Jesus' response is categorical and direct, grounded in both the nature of resurrection and the language of Scripture (following Mark 12:24-27, compare Matthew 22:29-32; Luke 20:34-38):

> You completely deceive yourselves, knowing neither the Scriptures nor the power of God! Because when they arise from the dead, they neither marry nor are they given in marriage, but are as angels in the heavens. But concerning the dead, that they

rise, have you not read in the book of Moses about the bush [Exodus 3:1-6], when God said to him, "I am the God of Abraham and the God of Isaac and the God of Jacob?" He is not God of the dead but of the living. You deceive yourselves greatly.

Jesus' second argument, the one from Scripture, is based on the encounter of Moses with God at the burning bush, and is easier to follow in its appeal both to the nature of God and to the evaluation of the patriarchs in early Judaism. By quoting from the Torah, Jesus challenges the Sadducees in their overall assumption that resurrection is not taught in the Scriptures, and he answers their hypothetical case drawn from the Torah with an actual statement from the Torah.

If God identifies himself with Abraham, Isaac, and Jacob, Jesus insists, it logically must be that in his sight, they live. And those three patriarchs—taken as foundations of the covenant with Israel—are indeed living principles of Judaism itself, in the ancient world and down to this day. These three patriarchs represent Israel as chosen in the case of Abraham (see Genesis 15), as redeemed in the case of Isaac (see Genesis 22), and as struggling to identity in the case of Jacob (see Genesis 32). Jesus does not produce an elaborate argument for the connection that links Abraham, Isaac, and Jacob with the deep identity of Israel. He makes that his assumption, just as he assumes the hearer is able to make such connections between the text of Scripture and the fulfillment of that Scripture within present experience.[3] Part of the challenge of understanding Jesus' attitude toward the Scriptures is that he saw their meaning more as fulfilled in the lives of those who heard him than as a significance produced by study or by being taught.

Jesus developed a logical argument from Scripture, using the assumption of fulfillment that was his trademark. His use of that logic makes his other claim in the passage, which appears first, seem all the bolder by comparison.

The direct comparison between people in the resurrection and angels is consonant with the thought that the patriarchs must live in the sight of God, since angels are normally associated with God's Throne (so, for example, Daniel 7:9-14). So, once the patriarchs are held to be alive before God, the comparison with angels is natural.

But Jesus' statement is not simply a theoretical assertion of the majesty of God, a majesty that includes patriarchs and angels in the heavenly court. Jesus also declares, confidently and without argument, what we can call a divine anthropology—the assurance that mortal people, by their constitution as human beings, will one day take their place in God's Glory. Jesus asserts that human relations, the usual basis of human society and the division of roles among people on the basis of their sexual identity, are radically altered in the resurrection. That claim of substantial regeneration and transcendence became a major theme among the more theological thinkers who followed Jesus, beginning with Paul.

But just before turning again to Paul, the first great interpreter of Jesus, we need to address a preliminary question. How is it that Jesus' position in regard to what resurrection involves is only spelled out in this *single* passage within the Gospels?

There is a general explanation that might be offered in this regard, but it is only partially satisfactory. The Synoptic Gospels are the best historical sources of Jesus' teaching that are available. They are closest in time to Jesus among all written records concerning him, whether in the New Testament or not. Yet although the Synoptic Gospels contain historical information, their intent is not to present a coherent history of events. Rather, they were designed in the interests of catechesis, for the preparation of converts for baptism, who were known in the ancient world as catechumens.

In contrast, the Gospel according to John has been known within Christianity since the second century as the spiritual Gospel, intended for mature believers in order to deepen their faith in the manner of a good sermon. What was in all probability the original ending of John states its purpose as upholding the faith of believers so that they might go on to have life in the name of Christ (John 20:31), while the introduction to Luke speaks of the things that the reader has only recently learned (Luke 1:1-4, and the verb is *katêkheo*). In between the initial preparation of catechumens and the advanced interpretation offered to those well beyond that point, a great deal of instruction naturally took place.

Teaching in regard to the resurrection perhaps belonged more to an intermediate level of instruction within early Christianity than to a preparatory or an advanced level. After all, Mark's Gospel relates no story of the appearance of the risen Jesus, but only the narrative of the women at the tomb (Mark 16:1-8). The silence of the women at the tomb is the last word in the Gospel, and it is an approving word. The Markan community is thereby instructed to maintain a reserve in the face of persecution. But it is very clear what that reserve is about: the young man at the tomb (Mark 16:6, 7) and Jesus himself at an earlier stage (Mark 8:31; 9:9, 31; 10:33, 34) leave no doubt that the full disclosure of Jesus' identity lies in his resurrection. As the Markan catechumen approaches the Paschal Mystery, when baptism will occur and full access to Eucharist extended for the first time, the door to the truth of Jesus' resurrection is opened in the Gospel, but actual entry to that truth awaits further (perhaps private) instruction.

Yet it will not do to invoke *only* a general explanation, in terms of the level of instruction involved, to account for the paucity of Jesus' own teaching regarding resurrection within the Gospels. After all, the topic is introduced, only then to be scantily addressed. Rather, there seems to have been a deliberate policy of esoterism in regard to resurrection. To some extent, the silence of the women in Mark after their experience at Jesus' tomb is an indication of this policy, and the possibility of persecution for belief in the resurrection of Jesus and all it involved helps explain this counsel of silence. But even these additional explanations seem inadequate. After all, the resurrection of Jesus is on any known reading the most obviously distinctive element in Christian teaching: how can there be a lack of cogency in providing for instruction on this point within the Gospels?

Mark's Gospel is a good initial guide to the problem. The young man at the tomb tells the women to tell the disciples and Peter that Jesus goes before them into Galilee, and that they will see Jesus there (Mark 16:7). That is, Peter is identified as the central named witness of Jesus' resurrection, but then no actual appearance to Peter is conveyed. Instead, the Gospel ends. Just as the Israelites could not see through the Glory that surrounded God at the time of Moses, the Gospels are deliberately elusive when it comes to dealing with Jesus as raised from the dead, because he also embodies the Glory that our world can barely accommodate.

"The Lord has risen, and has appeared to Simon" (Luke 24:34) is a declaration—widely recognized as primitive (compare 1 Corinthians 15:5)—that Luke alone relates. But here again, no actual story is attached to this statement. Instead, Luke then gives us, in addition to a recognizable but newly minted narrative of the visit to the tomb (Luke 24:1-12), the story of Jesus' appearance to the two disciples who were on their way to Emmaus (Luke 24:13-35).

The story about Jesus appearing to the disciples on their journey emphasizes that Jesus was not instantly recognizable to them, and he disappears once they finally *do* recognize him. Luke's text gives the theme of the narrative explicitly as Jesus' manifestation in the breaking of bread (v. 35). This occurs in the evidently liturgical context of the reminiscence of Jesus and the interpretation of Scripture (vv. 18-27).

Luke's narrative of Jesus' resurrection overall engages in paradox. Unlike Mark, Luke really provides a story of the *empty* tomb, because the women are described as entering and not finding Jesus' body (Luke 24:3). This change obviously anticipates that Jesus' resurrection involves the physical body that was buried. But alongside this account Luke's mysterious story about the disciples on their way to Emmaus portrays the resurrection in straightforwardly visionary and Eucharistic terms: Jesus is seen, but not recognized, then recognized, and no longer seen. The conflict with the story of the empty tomb is manifest, and all the more so as it is actually referred to by Cleopas in what he says to the stranger who turns out to be the risen Jesus (vv. 22-23); he dismisses the women's story as an idle tale.

Luke's Gospel is designed to resolve the paradox of the nature of resurrection to the extent that it can. The aim of resolution is reflected in the way the Gospel smoothes out the problem that would have been caused by telling the disciples to go to Galilee (as in Mark), since the risen Jesus appears only in the vicinity of Jerusalem in Luke. Instead, Luke's two men (rather than one young man) remind the women of what Jesus said *when he was in Galilee* (Luke 24:4-8). That enables the focus to remain Jerusalem, where the appearance to Simon occurred, and in whose vicinity the disclosure of the risen Jesus was experienced in the breaking of bread. Still, the actual appearance of Jesus to Simon is not related.

In that same Jerusalem itself, finally (never Galilee in Luke), Jesus appears in the midst of the disciples in the context of another meal, associated, in the manner of the story of the journey to Emmaus, with the interpretation of Scripture and the recollection of Jesus (Luke 24:36-49). Now, however, Jesus also shows his disciples that he is flesh and bone, not spirit, as the story of the empty tomb anticipates. He commissions them to testify to what they have experienced, instructing them to remain in Jerusalem until the power to become witnesses comes upon them. This fulfills the expectations raised by the empty tomb and is a triumph of harmonization: Jesus not only says he is flesh and bone but also shows his hands and his feet, offers to be touched, asks for food and eats it (vv. 38-43). Yet this physical emphasis is also synthesized with the visionary and liturgical idiom of what happened near and at Emmaus. This final appearance in Luke closes the Gospel. Leading his disciples out to Bethany, Jesus is taken up to heaven while he is in the act of blessing them (Luke 24:50-53).

Matthew, on the other hand, returns the focus to Galilee, *and to Galilee alone*, as the locus of the risen Jesus. Here Jesus himself encounters the women as they run to tell the disciples what the angel has said, and he tells them to instruct his brothers to go to Galilee (Matthew 28:10). The reference to "brothers" at this point, rather than to "disciples" (cf. 28:7), is apparently deliberate; the angel speaks to the women of disciples, while the risen Jesus now adds an injunction for a distinct group. After the story about the guard and the high priests (Matthew 28:11-15), however, the last passage in the Gospel according to Matthew, the appearance of

Jesus in Galilee, concerns only the eleven disciples. They see and worship (and doubt), receiving the commission to baptize all nations in the knowledge that Jesus is always with them.

In its own way, and centered in Galilee rather than in Jerusalem, Matthew achieves what Luke achieves: the appearances of the risen Jesus are visionary (and almost abstract), but the explanation of that vision is that his body was raised. The experience of the earthquake and the angel by the guards and their willingness to broadcast the lie (concocted by high priests and elders) that Jesus' body had been stolen (Matthew 28:2-4, 11-15), underscores that explanation. What remains startling about Matthew is the complete absence of direct reference to Peter in this context (compare Matthew 28:7 to Mark 16:7), although Peter is singled out for special treatment in the same Gospel (see Matthew 16:17-19).

Simon Cephas/Peter is held to be the fountainhead of this faith (as in 1 Corinthians 15:5), but the Synoptic Gospels simply do not convey a tradition of the appearance to Peter in particular. In addition, they are not consistent in their accounts of where Jesus appeared, even disagreeing in regard to whether Galilee or Jerusalem was the site.

John's Gospel places Peter and the other disciple whom Jesus loved, rather than Jesus' women disciples, at the empty tomb when the fact of the resurrection became known. The other disciple is said to have seen the tomb and to have believed, while Peter only looks into the tomb (John 20:1-10). Only then does Mary Magdalene see two angels and Jesus, but she does not recognize him at first and is forbidden to touch him: her commission is to tell the brothers that he goes to the father (John 20:11-18). Likewise, Jesus' purpose at this point is simply to go to the father, which presupposes that in what follows any descent from the father is uniquely for the purpose of appearing to the disciples. He appears among the disciples when the doors were shut for fear of the Jews, and provides Holy Spirit for forgiving or confirming sins (John 20:19-23). During the appearance, he shows his hands and his side in order to be recognized (20:20), which he does again in a second appearance, this time for the benefit of Thomas, and with the offer to touch his hands and his side (John 20:24-29). Obviously, the coalescing of the empty tomb and the visionary appearances has continued in John as it began in Luke, but the mystery of Simon Peter's role has not so far been resolved.

That resolution comes in the close of the present text of John, which is widely considered an addendum or annex (John 21). Here, Peter and six other disciples are fishing on the Sea of Galilee. The risen Jesus appears on the shore unrecognized, asking if they have anything to eat. They have not caught anything all night, but at Jesus' command they cast their net and catch more fish than they can pull up. The disciple whom Jesus loves recognizes Jesus and tells Peter who the stranger is. Peter leaps into the water and swims to shore, followed by the others in the boat. Jesus, whose identity none dares to ask, directs the preparation of breakfast from the 153 large fish that were caught. Finally, Peter himself is commissioned to shepherd the flock of Jesus.

This final appearance of the risen Jesus in John is the only appearance that features Peter, but even here, as in the story of what happened near and at Emmaus, Jesus is not immediately known. His identity is a matter of inference (see John 21:7, 12 and Luke 24:16, 31), because Glory is difficult for human beings to comprehend. This, of course, contradicts the expectation of an instantly recognizable Jesus, as if he simply survived after burial.

Both in the first century and today, some believers have presented Jesus' resurrection as if it were resuscitation. When Paul insisted that "flesh and blood can not inherit the kingdom of God" (1 Corinthians 15:50), he was not opposing an abstract proposition, but a belief in literalistic afterlife that he felt needed correction.[4] Indeed, he would seem on the face of the matter to contradict his own statement in 1 Thessalonians 4:13-18 that the dead will be raised and presented with the living, snatched up into the air for that purpose, so as always to be with the Lord. That literally physical belief in the general resurrection, which has been styled apocalyptic, influenced the portrayal of Jesus' resurrection in some texts and is most obvious in Luke's story of the empty tomb.

The accounts in Acts of how Paul encountered the risen Christ on the road to Damascus present a more complex picture. In chapter 9, those around Paul hear the voice but see nothing (Acts 9:7): the light blinds Paul, which is what brings him to Ananias and to baptism (Acts 9:3-18). In chapter 22, on the other hand, Paul is quoted as saying his companions saw the light but did not hear the voice (22:9), and that may be consistent with the sense of what he says later (Acts 26:12-18). A hasty reference to the materials of vision in Acts has led to the suggestion that the resurrection was associated with an experience of a heavenly light (or *Lichtglanz*, following the German wording of some interpreters).[5] The portrayal of Paul's vision of the risen Jesus in Acts surely warns us away from reducing the experience to a single sensation, and rather emphasizes the importance of being in the presence of the heavenly figure identified as Jesus, who commissions the recipient of the vision for a divine purpose. The "vision" or "appearance," so designated because the verbal usage "he was seen" (*ôphthê*) is preferred in the New Testament, involves the awareness—mediated by a variety of senses and apprehensions—that the risen Jesus is indeed present, and present so as to convey a divine imperative.

Those twin emphases, the identity of Jesus and the commissioning, underlie all stories of the actual appearance of the risen Jesus. Appearances of Jesus in the New Testament serve neither to console people generally about immortality nor to make an abstract point about God's eschatological victory.

Paul claims in his own writings that he has seen the Lord (1 Corinthians 9:1) and refers to that moment as when it pleased God to uncover his son in him (Galatians 1:15-16). The conviction of divine presence, identified with Jesus and inciting to a commission, defines the content of the experience that Jesus had been raised from the dead. That definition does justice to the narratives of Jesus' appearance in the Gospels, and to Paul's experience. "Vision," we might conclude, is the overall category of experience in which our sources place the resurrection of Jesus, but the experience was of his effectively divine and personal presence after his death, his Glory.

Jesus' own teaching about resurrection involved a refusal to grant an assumption of physical resuscitation (the continuity of sexual relationships), and in so doing disappointed literalistic expectations. There is little preserved of Jesus' teaching on this topic for the same reason that there is only an echo of Peter's experience of the risen Jesus: in both cases, the challenge to the literal assumptions that grew up around the story of the empty tomb was too great for many believers.

Paul's discussion of the issue of the resurrection in 1 Corinthians 15 represents his continuing commitment to the understanding of the resurrection that Jesus initiated, and an emphatic argument that the medium of human immortality, like the medium of God himself, is Glory. The particular occasion of his teaching is the apparent denial of the resurrection on the part of some people in Corinth (1 Corinthians 15:12b): "how can some of you say that there is no resurrection of the dead?"[6] Paul's address of that denial is first of all on the basis of the integrity of apostolic preaching. Indeed, Paul prefaces his question with the earliest known catalog of the traditions regarding Jesus' resurrection (1 Corinthians 15:1-11). That record makes it plain why so much variety within stories of the appearance of the risen Jesus in the Gospels was possible: reference is made to a separate appearance to Cephas, then to the Twelve, then to more than five hundred "brothers" (compare Matthew 28:10), then to James, then to "all the apostles," and then finally to Paul himself (vv. 5-8). The depth and range of that catalog is what enables Paul to press on to his first argument against a denial of the resurrection (15:13-14): "But if there is no resurrection of the dead, neither has Christ been raised; and if Christ has not been raised, then our preaching is empty and your faith is empty!"

Paul expands on this argument in what follows (1 Corinthians 15:15-19), but the gist of what he says in that section is as simple as what he says at first: faith in Jesus' resurrection logically requires an acknowledgement of the reality of resurrection generally. That may seem to be an argument entirely from hypothesis, until we remember that Paul sees the moment when belief occurs as the occasion of our reception of the Spirit of God (so Galatians 4:4-6):

> When the fullness of time came, God sent forth his Son, born from woman, born under law, so that he might redeem those under law, in order that we might obtain Sonship. And because you are sons, God sent the Spirit of his Son into your hearts, crying, "Abba! Father!"

Because the Spirit in baptism is the living Spirit of God's Son, Jesus' resurrection is attested by the fact of the initial experience of faith. The availability of Jesus' Spirit shows that he has been raised from the dead.

Paul's emphasis in this context on the spiritual integrity of the apostolic preaching, attested in baptismal experience, is coherent with Jesus' earlier claim that the Scriptures warrant the resurrection (since God is God of the living, rather than of the dead). Paul cites his own courage as an example of the hopeful attitude grounded in the resurrection of the dead: why else would Christians encounter the dangers that they do (1 Corinthians 15:30-32)?

Resurrection impinges directly upon what we conceive becomes of persons as we presently know them after they have died. And that, of course, will immediately influence our conception of people as they are now perceived and how we might engage with them. Paul therefore feels compelled to spell out his anthropology of resurrection, such that spiritual hope and the Scriptural witness are worked out within the terms of reference of human experience.

Precisely when he does that in 1 Corinthians 15, Paul develops a metaphysical anthropology. He does so by comparing people in the resurrection, not to angels, as Jesus himself had done, but rather *to the resurrected Jesus*. That comparison functions for Paul both because Jesus is preached as raised from the dead and because, within the experience of baptism, Jesus is known as the living source of the Spirit of God. Jesus as raised from the dead is the point of departure for Paul's thinking about the resurrection, and his analysis of the resurrection is much more systematic than Jesus'.

When Paul thinks of a person, any person, he conceives of a body as composed of flesh, physical substance that varies from one created thing to another (for example, people, animals, birds, and fish; 1 Corinthians 15:35-39). But in addition to being physical bodies, people are also what Paul calls a "psychic body," by which he means bodies with souls (1 Corinthians 15:44). Unfortunately, the phrase is wrongly translated in many modern versions, but its dependence on the noun for "soul" (*psukhe* in Greek) is obvious. The adjective does not mean "physical" as we use that word.[7] In other words, people as bodies are not just lumps of flesh, but they are also self-aware. That self-awareness is what makes them "psychic body."

In addition to being physical body and psychic body, Paul says people are—or can be, within the power of resurrection—"spiritual body" (1 Corinthians 15:44): "it is sown a psychic body, it is raised a spiritual body." Spirit in Paul's understanding is the means by which human beings can relate thoughts and feelings to one another and to God. The explanation of how this can be is explained earlier in 1 Corinthians (2:10-11). Paul develops his position starting from a passage in the book of Isaiah (64:4, which Paul quotes in 2:9), which speaks of things beyond human understanding, which God has readied for those who love him. Paul then goes on to say (2:10-11):

> God has revealed them to us through the Spirit; for the Spirit searches all things, even the depths of God. For who knows a person's concerns except the person's spirit within? So also no one has known God's concerns except the Spirit of God.

As Paul sees human relations, one person can only know what another thinks and feels on the basis of their shared "spirit."

"Spirit" is the name for what links one person with another, and by means of that link we can also know what God thinks and feels. The Spirit at issue in the case of God, Paul goes on to say, is not "the spirit of the world," but "the Spirit of God" (1 Corinthians 2:12): the means of ordinary, human exchange becomes in baptism the vehicle of divine revelation.

Paul's explanation in 1 Corinthians 2 is part of a complete anthropology, which is now spelled out further in 1 Corinthians 15. Jesus in the resurrection is the last Adam, a life-giving spirit (1 Corinthians 15:45), just as the first Adam was a living "being" or "soul" (the two words are the same in Greek, *psukhê*). Jesus is the basis on which we can realize our identities as God's children, brothers and sisters in Glory, and know the power of the resurrection. In so saying, Paul sets out a characteristic spirituality, predicated upon the regeneration of human nature. "Flesh" and "soul" become not ends in themselves but way stations on the course to "Spirit."

Paul provides an optimistic assessment of the human condition in 2 Corinthians 5:1-10 on the basis of his metaphysical anthropology: even as our present, earthly home is being dismantled, we have a heavenly dwelling prepared by God. The pledge of that trust, the hope of the resurrection, is the Spirit of God (v. 5). Here, speaking of the experience that brings assurance of resurrection, Paul is much less paradoxical than what is retained of Jesus' teaching, just as Paul is plainer than Jesus in his explanation of what is involved in the resurrection itself. Although Paul is not often called an optimist, chiefly because in terms of contemporary fashion he seems a perennially incorrect figure, his categorically bodily hope for the resurrection of the dead might be described as anything but pessimistic. This made Paul a foundational figure for the Christian understanding of life after death.

In his treatment of the resurrection, Origen of Alexandria (who lived between 185 and 253 C.E.) shows himself a brilliant exegete and a profound theologian. His contribution builds upon Paul's and provides a philosophical framework that has proven durable.

Origen sees clearly that, in 1 Corinthians 15, Paul insists that the resurrection from the dead must be bodily, and yet spiritual at the same time. Origen spells out the logical grounding of Paul's anthropology (*On First Principles* 2.10.1):

> If it is certain that we are to be possessed of bodies, and if those bodies that have fallen are declared to rise again—and the expression "rise again" could not properly be used except of that which had previously fallen—then there can be no doubt that these bodies rise again in order that at the resurrection we may once more be clothed with them.

But Origen equally insists upon Paul's assertion that "flesh and blood cannot inherit the kingdom of God" (1 Corinthians 15:50). There must be a radical transition from flesh to spirit, as God fashions a body that can dwell in the heavens (*On First Principles* 2.10.3).

Origen pursues the point of this transition into a debate with fellow Christians (*On First Principles* 2.10.3):

> We now direct the discussion to some of our own people, who either from want of intellect or from lack of instruction introduce an exceedingly low and mean idea of the resurrection of the body. We ask these men in what manner they think that the "psychic body" will, by the grace of the resurrection, be changed and become "spiritual"; and in what manner they think that what is sown "in dishonor" is to "rise in glory," and what is sown "in corruption" is to be transformed into "incorruption." Certainly if

they believe the Apostle, who says that the body, when it rises in glory and in power and in incorruptibility, has already become spiritual, it seems absurd and contrary to the meaning of the apostle to say that it is still entangled in the passions of flesh and blood.

Origen's emphatic denial of a merely physical understanding of the resurrection is especially interesting for two reasons.

First, Origen's confidence in his argument attests the strength of his conviction that a merely physical understanding of resurrection is "low and mean." The problem for him is not that physical resurrection is unbelievable, but that the conception is unworthy of the hope that faith speaks of. Origen's argument presupposes, of course, that a physical understanding of the resurrection was current in Christian Alexandria. But he insists, again following Paul's analysis and even repeating Paul's language, that the body that is raised in resurrection is continuous with the physical body in principle, but *different* from it in substance (*On First Principles* 2.10.3):

So our bodies should be supposed to fall like a grain of wheat into the earth, but implanted in them is the cause that maintains the essence of the body. Although the bodies die and are corrupted and scattered, nevertheless by the word of God that same cause that has all along been safe in the essence of the body raises them up from the earth and restores and refashions them, just as the power that exists in a grain of wheat refashions and restores the grain, after its corruption and death, into a body with stalk and ear. And so in the case of those who shall be counted worthy of obtaining an inheritance in the kingdom of heaven, the cause before mentioned, by which the body is refashioned, at the order of God refashions out of the earthly and animate body a spiritual body, which can dwell in heaven.

The direction and orientation of Origen's analysis is defined by his concern to describe what in humanity may be regarded as ultimately compatible with the divine. For that reason, physical survival is rejected as an adequate category for explaining the resurrection. Instead, Origen emphasizes the change of substance that must be involved.

Second, the force behind Origen's assertion is categorical. The resolution of the stated contradictions—"psychic"/"spiritual," "dishonor"/"glory," "corruption"/"incorruption"—involves taking Paul's language as directly applicable to the human condition. In the case of each contradiction, the first item in the pair needs to yield to the spiritual progression of the second item in the pair. That is the progressive logic of Origen's thought, here applied comprehensively to human experience.

For all that the transition from flesh to spirit is radical in his thought, Origen is also clear that personal continuity is involved. To put the matter positively, one is clothed bodily with one's own body, as we have already seen. To put the matter negatively, sins borne by the body of flesh may be thought of as visited upon the body that is raised from the dead (*On First Principles* 2.10.8), "in order that this very gloom of ignorance, which in the present world has taken possession of the inner parts of their mind, may in the world to come be revealed through the garment of their outward body."

Although Origen is consciously engaging in speculation at this point, he rejects the notion that the flesh is involved in the resurrection, even when biblical promises appear to envisage earthly joys (*On First Principles* 2.11.2):

> Now some men, who reject the labor of thinking and seek after the outward and literal meaning of the law, or rather give way to

their own desires and lusts, disciples of the mere letter, consider that the promises of the future are to be looked for in the form of pleasure and bodily luxury. And chiefly on this account they desire after the resurrection to have flesh of such a sort that they will never lack the power to eat and drink and to do all things that pertain to flesh and blood, not following the teaching of the apostle Paul about the resurrection of a "spiritual body."

Origen's reasons for rejecting such a millenarian view are both exegetical and theological. Paul is the ground of the apostolic authority he invokes, in a reading we have already seen. He uses that perspective to evaluate the Scriptures generally (*On First Principles* 2.11.3).

But Origen also deepens his argument from interpretation with a deeply theological argument. He maintains that the most urgent intellectual longing is the desire "to learn the design of those things which we perceive to have been made by God." This longing is as basic to our minds as the eye is to the body: constitutionally, we long for the vision of God (*On First Principles* 2.11.4).

Not only within the New Testament, but through the centuries of discussion that saw the meaning of resurrection discussed, Jesus' movement represents itself as a religion of humanity's spiritual regeneration. Humanity is regarded, not simply as a quality that God values, but as the very center of being in the image of God (Genesis 1:26-27). That center is precious to God because it is part of God's identity, and it is the basis upon which it is possible for human beings to enter the Kingdom of God, both now and eschatologically, so that they may join themselves to the Glory of God. Glory, on this understanding, is both the substance of God and the intended inheritance of mortal human existence.

Mindful Practice

Each of the prophetic resources we have encountered—the influences of Soul, Spirit, Kingdom, Insight, Forgiveness, Mercy, and Glory—find their roots in Jesus' practice. The roots that Jesus tapped into reached deep beneath him, into the ancient history of Israel, and far beyond Jesus' own religious culture, across the spiritual disciplines of the world's religions in many ages.

The prophetic powers Jesus identified are collective human strengths. They are the possession of no single religion or philosophy of life. Yet many religions and philosophies have made their signature contributions to human culture, and to the understanding of God, by putting prophetic perspectives into words and practices that can be understood across the boundaries that divide human communities in space and time. Although prophecy unites humankind, the articulation of its wisdom is best appreciated when we pay close attention to how specific prophets have transformed particular cultures.

The task of changing the world, of repairing and renewing what has been damaged or weakened, requires resilience as well as strength. Because prophetic resources lie within the human constitution, they are constantly renewable, and—as long as we remember to tap into them—inexhaustible. They belong to us, and once they are identified, we can rely on them.

The enduring strength of prophetic change, as distinct—for example—from a strategy for political reform or a plan for personal self-improvement, derives from its source. Political agendas and personal commitments can be noble, energetic, and productive. But their failures are at least as notable in human history as their successes. In contrast, prophetic change, which deploys the forces we have encountered, can act across ideologies and interests to produce sustainable transformations in the ways people live, engage with one another ethically, and understand themselves.

Many cultures have been repaired and renewed by relating Jesus' message to their unique conditions. American history is not an exceptional example of how prophetic change arises from the forces that Jesus identified within people, but it does provide striking examples of that transformation. By considering ways in which the transformational forces that Jesus set loose, and taught his disciples to identify when they prayed the Lord's Prayer, have permanently altered life in the United States, any person with a sense of history can see the difference between prophetic change and the relatively minor nips and tucks in the fabric of our common life which a dedication to ideology or interest can bring.

Our first chapter spoke of the *Tao te Ching* in order to introduce the fundamental integrity of the Soul. But we might have started nearer to home and on a much more modest level than the governing authority in China which Lao Tsu served. In 1754 an obscure Quaker and itinerant preacher named John Woolman published his essay, *Some Considerations on the Keeping of Negroes.* He developed a position against slavery that evolved out of his personal experiences as a clerk, a position that had involved him in the slave trade.

In his lifetime, John Woolman's success was limited, yet his personal journal remains of enduring value.[1] In his words and deeds, he foreshadowed what is arguably the most important transformation in American history, the end of slavery and its attendant racism, and he embodied the prophetic powers that we have encountered in this book.

When Woolman worked for a shopkeeper in his native Mount Holly, New Jersey, Woolman's employer asked him to write a bill of sale for a black woman. He wrote, "the thoughts of writing an instrument of slavery for one of my fellow creatures felt uneasy."[2] That unease, a product of the integrity of Woolman's Soul, in which he said he felt a sense "of the care and providence of the Almighty over his creatures in general," propelled him to oppose slavery, always seeking for ways to rectify its injustice. For him, that opposition was part and parcel of the basic identity of who he was.

Woolman's sense of himself was rooted, he said, in his devotion to God as the creator. And he believed that divine wisdom showed the connection among all human beings, inciting the awareness that, not only slavery, but any and all forms of oppression, derived from an abuse of the Spirit as revealed in creation, and in our minds. The depth of his opposition to slavery was rooted in his sense of who he was, but also—even deeper than that—in his discovery and experience of God's activity in the world. Soul brought him to an awareness of Spirit.

Woolman wrote of God with a surprising combination of immediate intimacy and systematic analysis:

> As he is the perfection of power, of wisdom, and of goodness, so
> I believe he hath provided that so much labour shall be necessary
> for men's support in this world as would, being rightly divided,

be a suitable employment of their time, and that we cannot go into superfluities, or grasp after wealth in a way contrary to his wisdom, without having connection with some degree of oppression and with that spirit which leads to self-exaltation and strife, and which frequently brings calamities on countries by parties contending about their claims.[3]

Slavery was only a part of the injustice that came when people forgot that "The Creator of the earth is the owner of it." One of Spirit's traits is her capacity to show up impulses opposed to God's love by the selfishness that contradicts divine Wisdom. Woolman grasped intuitively, and conveyed without explanation, just the connection between Spirit and Wisdom that we have encountered in our second chapter.

When Woolman turned to the issue of bringing up children, his emotions engaged him in purposeful dedication. Not content with any passing expression of affection, or the self-serving ambitions parents sometimes project onto their children, he wanted those who care for children to act from a steady regard for the purposes of justice overall, as revealed by God in creation.

Woolman urged parents to become "thoroughly instructed in the kingdom of God," in a way that accords with our discussion of the Kingdom.[4] A natural concern with justice, joining organically with righteous aims and actions, would move parents to the kind of healthy motivation that is not concerned with teaching children "the art of getting rich." Instead, on behalf of their children they should be "careful that the love of God and a right regard for all their fellow creatures may possess their minds."

Of course, *how* to relate God's justice, as revealed in his Kingdom, to the relations of the world in which people live daily, is a question answered over a lifetime. Any adequate response to that question is not an abstract or categorical answer but rather represents a state of the art at a given moment in one's life. Insight is what crafts that art, and Insight emerged clearly in Woolman's actions.

When Woolman was traveling, and being accommodated by fellow Friends who kept slaves, he sought for a way to make his opposition to slavery known without alienating his hosts. He came upon the policy that,[5] if he determined that what his hosts provided him to enjoy came from slave labor, he should pay the slaves concerned. He would either give money to his hosts to distribute or give it directly to the staff.

Payment of that kind conveyed Woolman's conviction that slavery and other forms of oppression arose from economic imbalance. Without directly condemning his hosts, he could nonetheless criticize their reliance on slaves and show how slaves could be treated as equals within a conventional economic exchange of payment for labor. Even the choice of whether to reimburse the host or to give directly to those who served marked a distinction, indicating both how far hosts might be trusted to use the payment to benefit their slaves and the extent to which slaves themselves should be encouraged to seek to be paid for their work. In a system in which slavery was endemic, a series of differing gestures needed to be developed in order to convey a single message of justice, and Woolman made many adjustments in expressing a single fundamental conviction during his active life.

In 1772, John Woolman visited England, where he also spoke out against slavery. During his lifetime, he saw no change in public policy, but Quaker teaching against slavery in nineteenth-century England *and* America influenced both countries to end the institution. In the year that he visited England, Woolman recalled in his journal a near-fatal attack of pleurisy and recollected a dream in which he heard the words of an angel that said, "John Woolman is dead."[6]

In his semi-conscious state, he dreamed of the exploitation of miners in their labor of taking silver out of the earth. When he recovered from his illness, he concluded that what had died was not his body but his will to enjoy unnecessary luxury. As he said, enjoying the forgiveness that gave him health again also provided a new resolve and a new discipline, that "I should take heed how I fed myself out of silver vessels."

Forgiveness and healing brought about a response of increased reliance on God and a stronger, more disciplined style of life. He also refused to use dyed clothing and avoided as many "superfluities" that he considered derived from slave labor *or* from commercial exploitation as possible.

To make his way across the Atlantic to England, Woolman resolved to book his passage in steerage, rather than accept a berth in a cabin. His decision reflected his characteristic thriftiness. After all, he had already reduced the size and scope of his business on several occasions in order to free himself for his ministry. More specifically, Woolman wanted to know at first hand what the condition of seaman was. As he put it, "I felt a draft in my mind toward the steerage."[7]

He was appalled by what he witnessed. The abuse of young seamen moved him as much as the plight of slaves and of American Indians, which he also detailed in his *Journal.* As he said, "Great reformation in the world is wanting!" He knew that commerce on the seas, as well as on land, was responsible for oppression, and he opened his heart in Mercy to the young men around him. That emotional tie was a constant, driving force.

Consistent and sensitive, John Woolman remained a beacon for the antislavery movement after 1772, the year of his death in York, England, from smallpox. The sense of purpose and quiet, consistent energy that drove him derived from a series of visions, which he usually referred to as "openings." In using that term, Woolman reached into the meaning of the term "apocalyptic," which literally means an uncovering.

To his mind, as in the Revelation of John, the last book of the New Testament (also known as the Apocalypse), an experience of the reality of God brings us to a surer place of Glory than the fleeting experiences of this world. He recorded his openings from very early in his life, as a schoolboy. He refers to some teasing from his companions and his withdrawal from them to read Revelation 22, where the text refers to the river of the water of life issuing from the Throne of God and from Christ as the Lamb of God. Woolman recollected:

> And in reading it my mind was drawn to seek after and long for that pure habitation which I then believed God had prepared for his servants. The place where I sat and the sweetness that attended my mind remains fresh in my memory.[8]

His mind's eye, rather than his vision of this world, kept his attention focused on a Glory that could not be taken away. That focus saw him through situations that would have brought lesser minds to despair.

Woolman's attention to what was present in his mind or what was beginning to stir there forms a thread that runs throughout his life and thought. Ralph Waldo Emerson spoke of Woolman as offering a philosophy of life and a clear insight, which Emerson even compared with the New Testament.[9] The philosophy

Emerson had in view was of the practical kind he himself preferred. But Emerson's remark about Woolman's "insight" is itself incisive, because Woolman developed Insight of a special kind to a high degree.

Insight, as we have seen, is a matter of crafting one's commitment to God's Kingdom into an art of life, of finding strategies for implementing God's will in a world whose spirit sometimes strives against God's. That same capacity can also be directed internally, so that the prophet becomes self-conscious of the various powers— "openings," as Woolman called them—operating within his mind.

"Mind" in exactly this understanding has been a pivotal concern in the literature of Gnosticism. Writing at the time he did, John Woolman can have known very little of that ancient literature, most of which was discovered after his death, and yet his agreement with its orientation shows how he aligned himself with classic understandings of prophecy.

In 1896, a manuscript was discovered in Egypt, entitled *The Gospel according to Mary*. That document has forever changed our understanding of Mary Magdalene[10] and of the role of mind in Gnosticism.

The Gospel according to Mary dates from early third-century Egypt, a text used among the prosperous landowners who sustained Gnosticism throughout the ancient period. Its Coptic language is key to Gnosticism's success in Egypt. The hieroglyphics of ancient Egypt were difficult to write and read, but Coptic put that language into the phonetic system of the Greek alphabet (with four extra characters). That innovation enabled people with leisure in rural Egypt to read and hear recitations of the world's wisdom in their own tongue. They became avid for philosophy, religion, and esoteric knowledge, and Gnosticism put them together in a way that assured its advance on Egyptian soil.

Following a pattern well known in several Gnostic Gospels, Jesus appears to his disciples after his death for an extensive period of time in *The Gospel according to Mary*. But his risen presence provides no solace, as it usually does in Gnostic literature. Instead, Jesus' appearance produces anguish. He insists that his followers act in ways that seem unnatural and perilous to them, commanding them to bring his message to the Gentiles. He does the same thing in the Gospel according to Matthew and the book of Acts, but in *The Gospel according to Mary* the disciples respond more fearfully than they do in the New Testament.

Jesus' disciples know that it was the Romans who killed him, and they realize all too clearly that if they obey him they court a similar fate. "If they did not spare him," they say, "how will they spare us?" (*Gospel according to Mary* 9.10). By the time this Gospel was written, its audience knew that the move to proselytize non-Israelites, although crucial to the emergence of Christianity, had also proved to be a deadly gambit for many of Jesus' closest followers.

Peter is a key figure in *The Gospel according to Mary*, as he is in the book of Acts; in both cases, contact with non-Jews is Peter's central concern. But *The Gospel according to Mary* presents a view of how the message of Jesus reached non-Israelites that contradicts the book of Acts, making Mary Magdalene rather than Peter the pivotal disciple who prompted that religious revolution.

The Gospel according to Mary goes its own way in portraying Peter as bewildered by Christ's command to approach people outside Israel. He needs to ask for Mary's advice, because he cannot understand why Jesus would tell him to court mortal danger. Mary *does* understand, so Peter turns to a woman's authority, despite his male antipathy toward doing so.

While Peter and his colleagues grieve at the prospect of the suffering that awaits them at Gentile hands, Mary intervenes, "greeting them all" and cajoling them to rely on God who "has prepared us and made us into men" (*The Gospel according to Mary* 9.19-20). The Magdalene emerges as an androgynous hero who strengthens the males in the apostolic company by means of the manhood, the visionary commitment to remain loyal to Jesus despite the risk of martyrdom, that she herself has received from Jesus. To be a "man" in this Gospel is to live in the realm of Spirit despite the threat of danger in the world of flesh.

Mary kisses her colleagues, "greeting them all." In Coptic as in Greek, the verb *aspazomai* implies a mouth-to-mouth embrace of fellowship. This gesture of trust among men and women signaled familial intimacy throughout the Mediterranean world. Men kissed men, women kissed women, women kissed men and vice versa. The "holy kiss" became a key Christian ritual, figuring centrally in both Catholic and Gnostic sources.

But the fact that the verb *aspazomai* is used here should not be misconstrued: it does *not* make Mary an especially sexual figure. Sadly, some modern translators have Mary "kissing" her colleagues, while elsewhere her male counterparts are portrayed as "greeting" each other, although exactly the same term is used. Loose, opportunistic translations of this kind perpetuate the Magdalene's caricature as our popular culture's favorite vixen.

Peter is at a loss in *The Gospel according to Mary* without Mary's guidance and strengthening, her special manhood. He and the apostles have given her a hearing because she is among the select company who experienced the resurrected Jesus. When she speaks of her own revelation, her discourse forms the core of *The Gospel according to Mary*, and its content authorizes the apostolic commission to Gentiles in Jesus' name, marking Christianity's emergence in the ancient world.

Mary Magdalene speaks very briefly in the text as it stands, because several pages containing her discourse have been physically removed. Yet even in its truncated form, her address offers the clearest evidence we have of how ancient Christianity and Gnosticism conceived of visionary experience. Her words vibrate with a simple grandeur and elegance (*The Gospel according to Mary* 10.6-20):

> I saw the Lord in a vision, and I said to him, "Lord, I saw you today in a vision." He answered and said to me, "You are privileged, because you did not waver at the sight of me. For where the Mind is, there is the treasure." I said to him, "Lord, now does he who sees the vision see it through the Soul or through the Spirit?" The Savior answered and said, "He sees neither through the Soul nor through the Spirit, but the Mind which is between the two—that is what sees the vision and is—"

Then the document breaks off for several pages.

Whatever Mary goes on to say in the missing part of the document, Peter and Andrew together rebuke Mary after her speech. Their anger—summed up in a rhetorical question—stems both from what she says and from what their paternalism considers to be her inferior gender (*The Gospel according to Mary* 17.9–19.1): "Has he revealed these things to a woman and not to us?" Mary's articulate insight in combination with her gender upsets Peter and his cohort. A woman had experienced a visionary breakthrough that permitted her to see Jesus' purpose in reaching out to Gentiles before Peter himself did. *The Gospel according to Mary* also understands that, in portraying the resurrection in visionary terms (as the perception of the "mind," not of physical eyes or ears or hands), Mary directly contradicted a growing fashion in Christianity that conceived of Jesus in the flesh resuscitated from the grave.

This Gospel reflects not only Mary's vision as she had articulated it from the first century but also the controversies of later periods, using the characters of Peter and Andrew to portray the reaction against Mary within the Catholic Church during the second and third centuries of the Common Era. As theologians became increasingly materialistic in their conception of how Jesus rose from the dead and how all believers were to be resurrected, Mary's vision fell into disfavor.

The Gospel according to Mary stood by Mary Magdalene's vision. Seeing Jesus here is unashamedly a perception of the "mind" (*nous* in both Greek and Coptic). Paul, who shared Mary's view of the resurrection, also articulated a theology of "mind" that agrees with this. As he said, "I will pray in the Spirit, but I will also pray in the Mind" (1 Corinthians 14:15). "Mind," for Paul as well as for *The Gospel according to Mary*, was the instrument of lucid vision.

"Mind," the term used in both Paul and *The Gospel according to Mary*, is the Hellenistic equivalent of "heart" (*libba*) in Aramaic. To appreciate the place of "heart" in the Aramaic language that shaped Mary's experience, we have to imagine thoughts flowing from our bodies in addition to feelings and affections, because the *libba* was the locus of insight as well as of emotions and sensations.[11] When Jesus promised that the pure in heart would see God (Matthew 5:8), that was a pledge of bodily transformation, not just cognition.

Paul shared Mary's conception of a transforming heart/mind as the key to human existence, but this conception was Mary's before it was Paul's. After all, he was a latecomer to the company of the apostles. Knowledge of God for Mary and Paul (as for the Gnostics) can only be spiritual, derived from divine revelation. Just as Paul says in 1 Corinthians 15, that resurrection is not achieved by flesh or even by Soul but only by Spirit, so he also insists that "the Soul-man (*psykhikos* in Greek) does not receive the things of the Spirit, for they are foolishness to him and he can't know, because they are discerned spiritually" (1 Corinthians 2:14). Quoting Isaiah again, Paul specifies the "Mind" (*nous* again) as the organ that perceives Spirit (1 Corinthians 2:16): "For who knows the Lord's Mind that will advise him? But we have Christ's Mind."

Paul and Mary agree on "mind" as the locus of revelation, and their agreement is completely coherent with their shared conception of how Jesus was raised from the dead. Mind for Paul discloses Spirit. Mind was also the visionary organ that powered the Magdalene's recognition of the risen Jesus, and it became a major concern of Gnosticism.[12] The importance of *The Gospel according to Mary* only comes out when we read it, not in isolation, but in its connection with the thought and practice of ancient Christianity as a whole. That principle, too often neglected in the study of Gnostic texts, permits us to perceive the power and continuing force of Mary's vision.

In Mary's vision, as in Jesus' and Paul's and John Woolman's, Mind is the awareness that links the prophetic powers and coordinates them into an active whole. All of these prophets, as the prophets before and after them, were not merely passive recipients of the divine influences they described. Rather, in each case, the prophet shapes those influences in a unique and unrepeatable way, reflecting his or her own character, temperament, and circumstances.

The capacity to be aware of the prophetic gifts within us, as individuals and as communities, lies within our Minds. Our choice to use our Minds to develop prophetic awareness is a matter of conscious decision. Prophecy, together with the prophetic power to repair and renew the world, has been with us since before history began to be written. Left to the chances of history, prophets have emerged sporadically, often to great effect, but more often than not as isolated figures who did not receive the hearing they deserved in their own time. But what if whole communities, formed by people inclined to Mindful discipline, treated prophecy as a human gift, conveyed by Spirit, rather than an unusual and random occurrence? St. Paul wrote to the Corinthians, "Pursue love, be zealous for spiritual things, and above all that you prophesy" (1 Corinthians 14:1). To him it seemed obvious that an awareness of God active among us should bring prophecy to the leading role in the guidance of communities. What is obvious to see, of course, is not always easy to do. To move from possibility to action will be the achievement of Mindful practice.

Perhaps the greatest benefit people can find is the capacity, freedom, and leisure to focus their Minds on the conditions they confront as individuals and communities. Most of the visionaries and prophets we have encountered in this book, including John Woolman and Mary Magdalene in this concluding chapter, chose their course in life deliberately. Difficulty and heroism was evidently involved, but they also exercised considerable choice in pursuing their paths towards the Glory they envisaged.

In the public arenas of politics and religion, some of the deepest principles inherent in the drama of being human are worked out.

But we should not imagine that, because John Woolman ultimately helped bring an end to slavery and because Mary Magdalene brought home to the apostles the truth of Jesus' resurrection, the prophetic principles we have discussed are only instanced in the great figures of history whose impact can be traced.

Jesus expected all his followers to pray, and he anticipated that they all would come to an awareness of the prophetic forces that inhabit each of us, because each of us is created in the image of God. The Mindful practice illustrated by John Woolman and Mary Magadalene is not their discipline alone but is the secure inheritance of all who follow Jesus.

In fact, sometimes the full power of Jesus' wisdom of prophetic mind comes out most forcefully, not in the steady strategies of public visionaries, but in the immediate, visceral responses of Mindful people who encounter tragedy. They act without regard to reputation or legacy, in honest reliance upon the forces at their disposal. Often, they exemplify the strength of the prophets.

One Sunday, while I was writing this book, I was getting ready to attend a long-planned event of inter-faith worship, involving colleagues who are expert practitioners in Buddhism, Hinduism, Islam, and Judaism. Our collaboration would, I hoped, bring me to a fresh awareness of the prophetic wisdom that underlies and constantly strengthens our great traditions. But the force of prophecy came to me on that day from a completely different and unexpected direction.

I never attended that service of common worship. Fortunately, another member of my staff was able to take my place. Even had she not been available, however, I would have had to send my apologies. Just before I was to leave my home to walk to the chapel on the campus of my college, a telephone call brought dreadful news.

A young, recently married professor had a friend call me from the hospital. He had just learned that his wife had been pronounced dead there.

As I drove to the hospital with my wife, we reviewed what we could piece together of what had happened. The young woman, pregnant and very near to her date of delivery, had been driving out of a service station, executing a left-hand turn. As she did that, another vehicle had run into her side of the vehicle. It was difficult to imagine how the baby could survive, and we understood that treatment to save the child was continuing, even after the mother had been pronounced dead.

Arriving at the hospital, we found many colleagues and friends gathered, all trying to help. The families of both the dead mother and our mourning colleague were also present in force, arriving constantly and calling in their plans to travel to our area. For several minutes, I was occupied more with those who were responding to the husband's loss than with the husband himself. At last, I sat down and prayed and talked alone with the grieving young man.

He spoke long and deliberately about his loss, but also about the enormous range of strengths and talents and emotions his wife had made him aware of, both within her and within himself. He spoke with a greater purpose than I usually find among the bereaved, and with quiet confidence. Then I found out why.

With a little, almost diffident smile, he said to me, "Would you like to meet my daughter?" The news I had not heard during our drive to the hospital was that an emergency cesarean section had proved a complete success. So the new father brought me into a room where his daughter slept, a nurse in attendance to survey her condition.

The baby seemed completely unharmed, and a little more alert than most newborns I have held in my arms. Beautiful dark hair already sprouted on her perfectly shaped head, and her puckering mouth gave every sign of healthy hunger. I blessed her as her father and I continued talking.

We wondered what his wife, a fine athlete, could possibly have done in the split seconds before impact to shield her daughter from the worst effects of the crash. We shall never know that. But what remained palpable was the act of will, of utter, Mindful concentration, that put her daughter first in her, the mother's, thoughts.

No broken life can simply be reassembled. There is no magical going back to the relatively pristine time before the accident. But I became aware from that moment that my colleague and friend had already identified the Mindful attention to the baby that would see him and his wider family, his friends and colleagues, and most importantly his newborn daughter herself, through unspeakable loss.

In this case, as in many other as a pastor, I found myself more recognizing the strength of renewal and solace that people already have within themselves, than giving them something from outside. Prophetic repair and renewal means that through the tears and the scars of an uncertain life, we can become vessels of divine light.

Not for a moment did my friend deny or minimize the loss of his young wife. But as he mourned, his mind steadied on the larger purpose—his wife's purpose—of nurturing his daughter. Jesus taught (Mark 10:15), "Amen I say to you, whoever does not receive the kingdom of God as a child, shall not enter into it." The daughter, born in tragedy, pointed both to the purpose of life and to the means of pursuing God's righteousness in an unjust world.

Following Jesus is not fundamentally a matter of religious affiliation, a way to feel better about yourself, or a means to acquire your eternal reward. The path we are on is meant to lead us closer to God's vision and purpose for this world—a world where, in our integrity and awareness of God's Spirit, we love righteousness, seek insight, heal with forgiveness, and love neighbors as ourselves. These ways are our glory as human beings in the present, and the prophetic promise is that this glory endures forever, for the living and for the dead.

Repair and renewal belong to the prophetic vocation Jesus has offered every human being, no matter how prominent or unnoticed the struggles involved may be. Our world is too complex, and its varying parts too numerous, for anyone to invent a comprehensive plan for its restoration. Yet at the same time, the world's myriad parts are too interrelated for any prophetic action, at any level, *not* to make a difference. Each of us acts in particular situations with a unique combination of talents, but our efforts, however local, influence the whole. What we do can alter the ways in which we understand ourselves and improve or diminish how our neighbors value their lives. Being human is itself a prophetic call.

Notes

To Begin

1. See *Rabbi Jesus: An Intimate Biography* (New York: Doubleday, 2000).

2. *Abraham's Curse: Child Sacrifice in the Legacies of the West* (New York: Doubleday, 2008).

3. For a comparative study of the three religions, see Jacob Neusner, Bruce Chilton and William Graham, *Three Faiths, One God: The Formative Faith and Practice of Judaism, Christianity, and Islam* (Boston and Leiden: Brill, 2003).

4. Written by Francis Fukuyama, the book was published by the Free Press in 1992.

1. Soul

1. *Nausea*, trans. Lloyd Alexander (New York: New Directions, 1959), 14–15.

2. This is the translation of the Tao te Ching by Lin Yutang, *The Wisdom of Laotse* (New York: Random House, 1948).

3. See Matthew 19:30; 20:8, 12, 14, 16, 27; Mark 9:35; 10:31, 44; Luke 13:30.

4. See Matthew 20:26, 28; 23:11; Mark 10:43, 45; Luke 22:27.

5. See Matthew 10:42; 18:1-5; Mark 9:33-37, 41; Luke 9:46-48; 22:26.

6. The cover is dated 10 September 2006.

7. T. D. Jakes, *Can You Stand to Be Blessed? Insights to Help You Survive the Peaks and Valleys* (Shippensburg, Pa.: Destiny, 1994), 13.

8. Book One, chapter I. See the translation by Henry Chadwick (Oxford: Oxford University Press, 2008).

9. *The Collected Works of Mahatma Gandhi* (Delhi: Ministry of Information 1994) vol. 86:75. The letter is dated March 20, 1945, and is addressed to G. D. Birla.

10. Thomas Merton, *Gandhi on Non-Violence: Selections from the Writings of Mahatma Gandhi* (New York: New Directions, 1965), 36.

11. This chronology is based upon a critical reading of the first-century historian Josephus, as well as of the Gospels and of Roman history. It extends the period in which Jesus was active beyond the implausibly brief period indicated by the Gospels, which follow a liturgical calendar, rather than the literal course of events. See *Historical Knowledge in Biblical Antiquity*, edited by Bruce Chilton, Jacob Neusner, and William Scott Green (Blandford Forum: Deo, 2007).

12. Celsus is quoted in Origen's work of the third century, *Contra Celsum* 2.24; see Henry Chadwick, *Contra Celsum: Translated with an Introduction and Notes* (Cambridge: Cambridge University, 1953). On the Aramaic idiom of the "cup," see Roger Le Déaut, "Goûter le calice de la mort," *Biblica* 43 (1962), 82–86. For a technical discussion of the Gethsemane scene and its sources, see Raymond E. Brown, *The Death of the Messiah*, The Anchor Bible Reference Library (New York: Doubleday, 1994), I:146–234.

13. The echo with the Lord's Prayer and its wording is deliberate in Mark; see Chilton, *Jesus' Prayer and Jesus' Eucharist: His Personal Practice of Spirituality* (Valley Forge: Trinity Press International, 1997).

14. The events are depicted by Roman historians, whose work I cited in *Rabbi Jesus*.

15. Johanna McGeary, "Mohandas Gandhi," *Time* 154.27 (1999): 118–23.

16. CNN (7 April 2008).

2. Spirit

1. See Chilton, *Abraham's Curse: Child Sacrifice in the Legacies of the West* (New York: Doubleday, 2008).

3. Kingdom

1. See Jacob Neusner, ed., *Religious Foundations of Western Civilization: Judaism, Christianity, and Islam* (Nashville: Abingdon Press, 2006).

2. For the original Aramaic of the prayer, see Bruce Chilton, *Jesus' Prayer and Jesus' Eucharist: His Personal Practice of Spirituality* (Valley Forge: Trinity Press International, 1997).

3. See Bruce Chilton, *Jesus' Baptism and Jesus' Healing: His Personal Practice of Spirituality* (Harrisburg, Pa.: Trinity Press International, 1998), 58–97 and Scot

McKnight, *A New Vision for Israel: The Teachings of Jesus in National Context*, Studying the Historical Jesus (Grand Rapids: Eerdmans, 1999), 15–69.

4. Roy P. Basler, ed., *The Collected Works of Abraham Lincoln* (New Brunswick N.J.: Rutgers University Press, 1953).

5. David Flusser, *Die rabbinischen Gleichnisse und der Gleichniserzähler Jesu* (New York: Peter Lang, 1981).

6. See Chilton, *Redeeming Time: The Wisdom of Ancient Jewish and Christian Festal Calendars* (Peabody, Mass.: Hendrickson, 2002).

7. That doesn't mean it has been doubted or even denied, but that says more about the liking of some scholars for revisionism than about the historical Jesus. See *Rabbi Jesus* for a discussion of the incident.

8. Christopher H. Evans, *The Kingdom Is Always But Coming: A Life of Walter Rauschenbusch*, Library of Religious Biography Series (Grand Rapids: Eerdmans, 2004).

4. Insight

1. Barbara Stoler Miller, *The Bhagavad-Gita: Krishna's Counsel in Time of War* (New York: Bantam, 1986), XI.6

2. Ibid., I.28–32, 36.

3. Ibid., II.26–27, 30.

4. See J. T. F. Jordens, "Gandhi and the *Bhagavadgita*," *Modern Indian Interpreters of the Bhagavadgita*, ed. Robert N. Minor (Albany: State University of New York Press, 1986), 88–109, from which quotations from Gandhi are taken, as well as M. K. Gandhi, *Gita, My Mother*, ed. Anand T. Hingorani (Bombay: Bharatiya Vidya Bhavan, 1965); *Gandhi and the Gita*, ed. J. I. [Hans] Bakker (Toronto: Canadian Scholars Press, 1993).

5. See Christopher D. Marshall, *Beyond Retribution: A New Testament Vision for Justice, Crime, and Punishment* (Grand Rapids: Eerdmans, 2001); Robin W. Lovin, *Christian Ethics: An Essential Guide* (Nashville: Abingdon Press, 2001).

6. See T. W. Manson, *The Teaching of Jesus* (Cambridge, England: Cambridge University, 1955), 76–80; Bruce Chilton, *A Galilean Rabbi and His Bible: Jesus' Own Interpretation of Isaiah* (London: SPCK, 1984), 90–98; Craig A. Evans, *To See and Not Perceive: Isaiah 6:9-10 in Early Jewish and Christian Interpretation*, Journal for the Study of the Old Testament Supplement Series 64 (Sheffield, England: Sheffield Academic Press, 1989). A recent attempt by Michael Goulder to deny the similarity between Jesus' saying and the Isaiah Targum is refuted in Bruce Chilton and

C. A. Evans, "Jesus and Israel's Scriptures," *Studying the Historical Jesus: Evaluations of the State of Current Research*, New Testament Tools and Studies 19 (Leiden: Brill, 1995), 281–335, 300–304. Cf. M. D. Goulder, "Those Outside (Mk. 4:10-12)," *Novum Testamentum* 33 (1991): 289–302.

5. Forgiveness

1. See Bruce Chilton, *Mary Magdalene: A Biography* (New York: Doubleday, 2005).

2. Known as Gamaliel II, to distinguish him from Gamaliel of the time of Paul, who was the grandfather of Gamaliel II.

3. Material regarding the *chasidim* was conveniently gathered together by George Foot Moore, *Judaism in the First Centuries of the Christian Era* (Cambridge, Mass.: Harvard University Press, 1927), I:377–78; his work that has been repeated many times in the secondary literature. Sometimes, however, the similarities among the *chasidim* have been stressed to the point that they all begin to look alike, Jesus included. Moore's work remains useful, not only in bringing the material together with a good, critical eye but in avoiding the hasty aggregation of all the *chasidim* into a single model.

4. Mary Magdalene is not even named in Luke's Gospel until the next chapter. For a treatment of Mary throughout Christian tradition, see *Mary Magdalene: A Biography*.

5. Oil, because it was a fluid, was held particularly to convey uncleanness so that having pure oil in one's household was vital to maintaining the laws of *kashrut*. In his histories, Josephus refers to the purity of Galilean oil in contrast to Hellenistic products; *Life*, 74–75; *Jewish War*, 2.591–592; *Antiquities*, 12.120.

6. Mishnah Qiddushin 4:1-2 makes these rules explicit:

> Ten descents came up from Babylonia: (1) priest, (2) Levite, (3) Israelite, (4) impaired priest, (5) convert, (6) freed slave, (7) *mamzer*, (8) *Netin*, (9) silenced [*shetuqi*], and (10) foundling. Priest, Levite, and Israelite intermarry among one another. Levite, Israelite, impaired priest, convert, and freed slave intermarry one another. Convert, freed slave, *mamzer*, *Netin*, silenced, and foundling all inter-marry among one another. These are silenced: everyone who knows his mother but does not know his father. Foundling is one who retrieved from the market and knows neither his father nor his mother. Abba Saul called a "silenced" [*shetuqi*] "to be examined" [*beduqi*].

For an explanation of these rules, see Bruce Chilton, "Recovering Jesus' *Mamzerut,*" *Ancient Israel, Judaism, and Christianity in Contemporary Perspective: Essays in Memory of Karl-Johan Illman,* eds. Jacob Neusner, Alan J. Avery-Peck, Antti Laato, Risto Nurmela, Karl-Gustav Sandelin (Leiden: Brill, 2005); *Rabbi Jesus,* 12–22, 64–69, 133–34.

7. Trust or confidence is implicated in the Greek and Hebrew terms for "faith."

8. Cf. Bruce Chilton, *A Galilean Rabbi and His Bible: Jesus' Use of the Interpreted Scripture of His Time,* Good News Studies 8 (Wilmington, Del.: Glazier, 1984), 117–23.

9. See Bruce Chilton, *Rabbi Paul: An Intellectual Biography* (New York: Doubleday, 2004).

10. See C. F. D. Moule, *Forgiveness and Reconciliation: Biblical and Theological Essays* (London: SPCK, 1998).

6. Mercy

1. Digha Nikaya, ii.1–19, within the Pali Tipitaka, the canon of Theravada Buddhism, which is also basic within Mahayana Buddhism.

2. *Love and Sympathy in Theravada Buddhism* (Delhi: Motilal Banarsidass, 1980).

3. Khuddaka Patha, 232–35.

4. *Rabbi Jesus* develops the chronology followed here.

5. See Jeremias Jeremias, *The Parables of Jesus,* trans. S. H. Hooke (London: SCM, 1976), 136–39.

6. See C. F. D. Moule, "'…As we forgive…': A Note on the Distinction between Deserts and Capacity in the Understanding of Forgiveness," in *Essays in New Testament Interpretation* (Cambridge, England: Cambridge University Press, 1982), 278–86, 282–84. See also J. A. Sanders, "Sins, Debts, and Jubilee Release," in C. A. Evans and J. A. Sanders, *Luke and Scripture: The Function of Sacred Tradition in Luke-Acts* (Minneapolis: Fortress, 1993), 84–92.

7. Cf. Bruce Chilton and J. I. H. McDonald, *Jesus and the Ethics of the Kingdom,* Biblical Foundations in Theology (London: SPCK; Grand Rapids: Eerdmans, 1987), 31–43.

8. Cf. F. Hauck, *Theological Dictionary of the New Testament* 5, trans. G. W. Bromiley (Grand Rapids, Eerdmans, 1978), 559–66.

9. D. H. Lawrence, *Apocalypse* (Cambridge, England: Cambridge University Press, 1980).

10. Joseph A. Fitzmyer supports the traditional surmise that Philemon came

from Colossae but agrees that he traveled, making Ephesus the likely place of his acquaintance with Paul; *The Letter to Philemon: A New Translation with Introduction and Commentary*, The Anchor Bible 34C (New York: Doubleday, 2000), 12–13.

11. That hymnic quality is beautifully represented in English by the King James Version, which I cite here. For a discussion of the significance of the passage, see James D. G. Dunn, *The Theology of Paul the Apostle* (Grand Rapids: Eerdmans, 1998), 244–52.

12. Paul here paraphrases Isaiah's prediction (45:23) of how *God* will be acknowledged.

7. Glory

1. See Bruce Chilton, *The Kingdom of God in the Teaching of Jesus* (London: SPCK and Philadelphia: Fortress, 1984). For discussion since that time and the significance of eschatology, see Bruce Chilton, *Pure Kingdom: Jesus' Vision of God*, Studying the Historical Jesus 1 (London: SPCK; Grand Rapids: Eerdmans, 1996).

2. See Bruce Chilton, *The Temple of Jesus: His Sacrificial Program Within a Cultural History of Sacrifice* (University Park: Pennsylvania State University Press, 1992), 82. The Sadducees' position is attributed to them only by unsympathetic observers, Josephus (War 2 § 165-166) and various Christians (Mark 12:18-27; Matthew 22:23-33; Luke 20:27-38; Acts 23:6-8). Targumic texts as late as the Middle Ages continue to refer to the denial of resurrection within the dispute between Cain and Abel, which is developed at Genesis 4:8.

3. For Jesus' characteristic attitude toward Scripture, see Bruce Chilton, *A Galilean Rabbi and His Bible: Jesus' Use of the Interpreted Scripture of His Time* (Wilmington: Glazier, 1984); also published with the subtitle, *Jesus' Own Interpretation of Isaiah* (London: SPCK, 1984).

4. The disagreement with some in Corinth is not over whether there is to be a resurrection, but what resurrection is to involve. See A. J. M. Wedderburn, *Baptism and Resurrection: Studies in Pauline Theology against Its Graeco-Roman Background*, Wissenschaftliche Untersuchungen zum Neuen Testament 44 (Tübingen: Mohr, 1987), 35–36. Given Paul's form of words in 1 Corinthians 15:29, the tendency to make any disagreement about resurrection into a denial is evident.

5. For a suitably cautious assessment, see Peter Carnley, *The Structure of Resurrection Belief* (Oxford: Clarendon, 1987), 240–42.

6. For a survey of attempts to explain this statement, see Wedderburn, 6–37. He comes to no finding regarding what view Paul meant to attribute to some

Corinthians, but he seems correct in affirming that a simple denial on their part (despite the form of words Paul uses) is unlikely. More probably, Paul was dealing with people who did not agree with his teaching of a bodily resurrection.

7. Although that is a simple point, it apparently requires some emphasis. Scholars of Paul routinely assert that Paul is speaking of some sort of physical resurrection, when that is exactly what Paul denies.

Mindful Practice

1. Phillips P. Moulton, ed., *The Journal and Major Essays of John Woolman,* (Richmond, Ind.: Friends United Press, 2007), from the earlier edition in the series, *A Library of Protestant Thought* (New York: Oxford University Press, 1971).

2. In the *Journal,* these statements appear at the end of the entry for 1720–1742.

3. This quotation comes from the entry for 1761–1763, the statement at the close of the paragraph from Woolman's essay "A Plea for the Poor" (which was written in 1763–1764, although not published until after his death, in 1793).

4. Woolman's statement appears in chapter fourteen of "A Plea for the Poor."

5. He describes his attitude in his *Journal* entry for 1757.

6. Entry in the *Journal* for 1772.

7. In the entry for 1772, which is also where the quotation in the next paragraph comes from.

8. This is part of the initial entry in the *Journal.*

9. He also said, "I find more wisdom in these pages than in any other book written since the days of the apostles." The Moulton edition of the *Journal* discusses Emerson's views in its introduction.

10. For a fuller discussion, see Bruce Chilton, *Mary Magdalene: A Biography* (New York: Doubleday, 2005).

11. For example, Job conceives of his own death as climaxing in a moment of insight. When his flesh is stripped away, he shall nonetheless see God, as his redeemer. The removal of the flesh—even by the painful, steady drip of mortal suffering—brings Job to the moment he can perceive God with all that he has left of his being, his "heart" (see Job 8:10; 19:23-27). For Job and for the Prophets, in fact for Hebrew and Aramaic speakers generally in the ancient world, the heart was what a person thought and felt with. Modern English still preserves a bit of this conception; we speak of loving with one's whole heart, and the feeling of love is often experienced in one's chest and gut, whatever we may claim to know of psychology and physiology.

12. The Nag Hammadi Library, the principal source of ancient Gnostic writings, actually begins with *The Prayer of the Apostle Paul,* which addresses Christ by saying "You are my Mind: bring me forth! You are my treasure: open for me!" (I.1.6–7). This agrees with *The Gospel according to Mary.* There are also echoes of Mary's conception in *The Sophia of Jesus Christ* (III.4.98.9–22); *The Dialogue of the Savior* (III.126.16–23; III.134.20–135.5); *The Thunder, Perfect Mind* (VI.2.18.9–10); *The Paraphrase of Shem* (VII.1.5–15); *The Second Treatise of the Great Seth* (VII.2.64.9); *The Teachings of Silvanus* (VII.4.103.1–10). Wherever possible, I have followed the system of citation presented in *The Nag Hammadi,* Library in English, ed. James M. Robinson (San Francisco: Harper & Row, 1978). This is the most widely used translation of the ancient library of Gnostic books discovered in Egypt in 1945, and it also includes *The Gospel according to Mary.*